THE ECONOMIC VALUE
OF CAREERS GUIDANCE

THE ECONOMIC VALUE OF CAREERS GUIDANCE

John Killeen, Michael White and A.G. Watts

Policy Studies Institute in association with
National Institute for Careers Education and Counselling
London 1992

**The publishing imprint of the independent
POLICY STUDIES INSTITUTE
100 Park Village East, London NW1 3SR
Telephone: 071-387 2171; Fax: 071-388 0914**

NICEC
National Institute for Careers Education and Counselling
Hatfield Polytechnic
Hertford Campus
Mangrove Road
Hertford, Herts SG13 8QF
Tel: 0992 558451

© Crown copyright 1992. Published by permission of the Controller of Her Majesty's Stationer Office.

All rights reserved. No part of this publication may be reproduced, stored in a rtetrieval system or transmitted, in any form or by any means, electronic or otherwise, without the prior permission of the Department of Employment.

The views expressed in this report are those of the authors and not necessarily of those of the Department of Employment or any other Government organisation or department.

ISBN 0 85374 499 8
PSI Report No. 702

A CIP catalogue record of this book is available from the British Library.

1 2 3 4 5 6 7 8 9

How to obtain PSI publications
All book shop and individual orders should be sent to PSI's distributors:

BEBC Ltd
9 Albion Close, Parkstone, Poole, Dorset, BH12 3LL

Books will normally be despatched in 24 hours. Cheques should be made payable to BEBC Ltd.

Credit card and telephone/fax orders may be placed on the following freephone numbers:
FREEPHONE: 0800 262260   FREEFAX: 0800 262266

Booktrade Representation (UK & Eire)
Book Representation Ltd
P O Box 17, Canvey Island, Essex SS8 8HZ

PSI Subscriptions
PSI Publications are available on subscription.
Further information from PSI's subscription agent:

Carfax Publishing Company Ltd
Abingdon Science Park, PO Box 25, Abingdon OX10 3UE

Laserset by Stanford Desktop Publishing Services, Milton Keynes
Printed in Great Britain by Chameleon Press, London

Contents

Preface: The Policy Context   i
A.G. Watts

Section One: General Introduction   1
John Killeen and Michael White

Section Two: The Potential of Guidance: Ideas from Economics   12
Michael White

Section Three: The Evidence   39
John Killeen

Section Four: The Future of Guidance Evaluation   77
John Killeen and Michael White

Notes   88

References   97

This work was produced under contract with the Employment Department; the views expressed are those of the authors and do not necessarily reflect those of the Employment Department or of any other Government Department.

Preface: The Policy Context
A.G. Watts

Careers guidance services are sometimes asked to justify their activities in terms of the economic benefits which their activities yield. Measuring such benefits poses considerable difficulties. It is however important that efforts are made to clarify these difficulties, to resolve them where necessary, and to produce responses which are satisfactory as can be achieved within the limits of what is technically feasible and professionally defensible.

In policy terms, guidance services serve a number of different constituencies. In addition to *individuals*, they offer benefits to *education and training providers*, in increasing the effectiveness of their provision by helping learners to be linked to programmes which meet their needs. They also offer benefits to *employers*, in helping potential employees to come forward whose talents and motivations are matched to the employer's requirements. Finally, they offer benefits to *governments*, in making maximum use of the society's human resources. In particular, guidance services can play a significant role in fostering *efficiency* in the allocation and use of human resources, and in fostering *social equity* in access to educational and vocational opportunities (Watts *et al.*, 1988).

It is primarily for these reasons that guidance services are supported from the public purse. At the same time, those involved in the provision of such services have consistently argued that their *primary* client must be the individual. There are good practical as well as ethical reasons for this, not the least of which is the point that guidance services can only serve the interests of their secondary clients if they retain the confidence and trust of the individuals with whom they are working – whose interests must accordingly be given primacy.

Recently, careers guidance has been given a higher priority on the public-policy agenda. This policy interest has stemmed in significant measure from the Confederation of British Industry's seminal report *Towards a Skills Revolution* (CBI, 1989). Concerned about Britain's need to improve skill levels in order to compete in world markets, the CBI suggested that one of the main criticisms of the current education and training system was that it had always given the needs of providers higher priority than the needs of individuals. It accordingly argued that the way forward was to 'put individuals first' and to encourage them to develop their skills and knowledge throughout their working lives. The CBI saw this notion of 'careership' as a concept which should be applicable to all individuals, and in particular it recommended a system of credits which would give individuals a publicly-funded right to post-compulsory education and training and control over the form it should take. It viewed effective careers guidance as the essential means of ensuring that such individual decisions were well-informed, and proposed that careers guidance required a 'new rationale, reinvigoration and extra investment' (p.23).

The Government White Paper *Education and Training for the 21st Century* (DES/DE, 1991) was strongly influenced by the CBI report and gave government support to many of the ideas contained in it. It announced the Government's intention to implement a system of training credits for young people so that by 1996 it would cover all 16/17-year-olds leaving full-time education. It also proposed a number of measures for developing 'better careers advice'.

Within these policy developments there are two distinct concepts at work (Watts, 1991). Both attempt to relate careers guidance more closely to market principles, but in very different ways. One is the notion of *guidance as market maker*. The basic notion here is that guidance can be viewed as a tool for making markets work, ensuring that the supply-side has access to market information and is able to read and take account of market signals. This provides in principle a rationale for publicly-funded but client-centred guidance services which can invoke Adam Smith (1776) himself: in enabling individuals to pursue their best interests, guidance services can – via Adam Smith's 'invisible hand' – promote the interests of society too.

The other notion is that of introducing a *market in guidance*: of exposing guidance services themselves to market forces. Thus the 1991 White Paper proposed, among other options, to enable Local Education Authorities to contract out the Careers Service through competitive tendering if they wished; it also proposed to take reserve powers to require such tendering, if experience showed this to be a good way of managing the service. Meanwhile, some of the new Training and Enterprise Councils have become interested in the notion of developing counselling vouchers for adults, associated with the idea of encouraging competition between guidance providers (Full Employment UK, 1991): the Employment

The Policy Context

Department's 'Gateways to Learning' initiative offers encouragement to such approaches.

There are clearly tensions and potential contradictions between these two notions. The notion of guidance as market-maker implies that it is in the public interest for there to be universal access to guidance; the notion of a market in guidance, on the other hand, may limit the take-up of guidance to those who can see its benefits and can afford it (or be given vouchers for access to it). Again, the notion of guidance as market-maker emphasises the importance of neutrality in the guidance that is offered; the notion of a market in guidance may prejudice such neutrality, depending on who is paying.

It is worth noting in this respect that in Germany, which has been widely viewed as an influential model in relation to many aspects of education and training provision, the notion of introducing a market in guidance has been firmly rejected. Vocational guidance and placement is the sole and exclusive responsibility of the Bundesanstalt für Arbeit: a self-governing legal body financed by contributions from employers and employees through the social pensions insurance scheme, and controlled by the three social partners – employers, unions and government – which in effect ensure that their respective vested interests are balanced and that the individual's interests are given primacy. Other institutions – including schools and universities – are prohibited from offering individual vocational guidance; private agencies are not permitted (Busshoff and Heller, 1988). The rationale is to help individuals to realise their basic right, enshrined in the German constitution, of free vocational choice. From the market perspective, it views careers guidance firmly as a public good, operating as a market-maker.

Within Britain, the debate about how guidance services should be financed has yet to be resolved. Most services for young people are publicly provided. There has however been a lack of consensus about the extent to which guidance services for adults should be paid for by individuals, by employers or by government. The failure to achieve a consensus has seriously inhibited the development of such services, and yet such development is widely recognised as becoming more and more urgent from a 'market-maker' viewpoint as the pace of occupational change quickens and as the need for flexibility in the labour market grows. This mirrors the way in which the lack of a consensus about funding has inhibited the development of education and training provision for adults.

In his recent consultation document *Learning Pays*, Sir Christopher Ball suggests that education and training should be viewed in relation to three stages of learning: the *foundation* stage, up to the end of compulsory schooling, designed to inculcate the habit of learning; the *formation* stage, covering the first few years of post-compulsory education and training, designed to inculcate work-place readiness; and the *continuation* stage, covering the rest of life, based on independent learning. He suggests that the foundation stage should be financed by government; that the state should also take the leading responsibility in providing the means for all to complete their formation stage; but that the continuation stage should be left to the market and funded privately (Ball, 1991). This model is put forward chiefly as a stimulus for structuring the debate about the funding of education and training. It raises the question of whether policy in relation to guidance – the importance of which the Ball report also underlines (p.31) – should be the same as that adopted in relation to education and training. Or should publicly-provided guidance services be regarded as an appropriate means of supporting progression of learning throughout the individual's career, including – on the 'market-maker' argument – the operation of market principles where these are applied in relation to education and training provision?

The rest of this monograph does not attempt to resolve these debates. It does however provide a review and analysis from an economic perspective of the ways in which careers guidance can contribute to the workings of the labour market, and of the evidence available on its impact in this respect. In doing so, it aims to provide a stronger theoretical and evidential base than has been available hitherto on which such debates can draw.

The monograph has been a joint collaboration between two bodies: the National Institute for Careers Education and Counselling, which is concerned with developing theory, informing policy and enhancing practice in relation to guidance work in educational institutions and in work and community settings; and the Policy Studies Institute, which is an independent research organisation aiming to inform public policy by establishing objective facts. We would like to express our thanks to the Employment Department for funding the project, and also to the members of the NICEC Research Seminar – notably Ruth Hawthorn, Bill Law and Jim Sampson (Florida State University, USA) – for their help in the early stages of the work. The monograph is of course the responsibility of its authors and does not necessarily reflect the views of any government department.

Section One: General Introduction
John Killeen and Michael White

The papers which follow perform three tasks:
(i) To analyse the public economic benefits which may *potentially* arise from guidance.
(ii) To review the evidence for supposing that guidance already results in economic benefits to individuals, employers, and the providers of education and training.
(iii) To recommend how future research should be conducted, in order to place our judgments of all of these matters on to a surer footing.

In our Introduction, we shall define several of the key terms. The most obvious place to begin is with 'guidance' itself.

A. What is Guidance?
There is no one generally accepted definition of careers guidance. The activities carried out by professional people offering guidance, such as careers teachers in schools, careers officers, or educational guidance practitioners, have been said to include informing, advising, counselling, assessing, enabling, advocating and feeding-back (UDACE, 1986); to these have been added teaching, networking, managing, and innovating/systems change (SCAGES, 1991). But such a list makes the task of defining guidance more complex, if anything. Our purpose here is to look at guidance from the viewpoint of its beneficiaries, and to ask 'What does guidance *achieve*?'.

From this viewpoint, guidance can perhaps be most simply defined in terms of its focus and its purpose. The focus of guidance (as we are considering it) appears to be individual decisions or choices in regard to the labour market. This entails, but is not confined to, decisions or choices as between employment statuses, occupations and employers. As a matter of definition, guidance for certain other decisions, such as those referring to education for 'leisure' purposes, is excluded, although in practice this line might be difficult to draw.

The emphasis on *individual* choice in this statement does not imply that guidance can only be offered on a one-to-one basis: even mass guidance (for example, offered by TV or radio) can affect individuals. In addition, individuals do not make choices in a social vacuum. In particular, their family circumstances are likely to weigh heavily with them. Similarly, emphasis on *decision* or *choice* does not limit the definition to discrete steps or sharply defined commitments. Decisions or choices may take the form of processes which go on over extended periods. They may also be considered as sequences spread out in time, involving many subsidiary steps. People may not so much 'make choices' as move into positions, or adopt stances, which subsequently affect what they do when they come to 'choice points'. Practitioners of guidance are familiar with this general idea, often formulated from a developmental perspective (e.g. Gottfredson, 1981). So guidance can be a process operating, intermittently or continuously, over a period.

Relative to this type of choice process, guidance can be understood quite simply as the provision of any purposive assistance for the benefit of individuals. In plain words, guidance consists in helping people to make decisions (or to move through choice processes); moreover, the help is provided intentionally, rather than incidentally or accidentally. This distinguishes guidance from the mere existence of information in the individual's environment. What is distinctive about guidance is that it is not merely a bundle of information. It is an effort to help people by, for example, organising or structuring information, selecting from it, teaching people how to think through the issues, and to come to decisions.

B. Who Offers It?

It would be unhelpful and confusing to restrict our definition of guidance so as to exclude some of its actual or possible sources or, for that matter, some of its actual or possible media. Anyone who pursues the purpose we have outlined, through any medium, offers guidance. This means that parents, friends, broadcasting organisations and employers all can (and, in point of fact, do) provide guidance. It also means that guidance may come in the form of written material, radio or television programmes, or computer software. But this said, it may be helpful to the reader if we sketch out what are sometimes called the 'formal'[1] sources of guidance. These include: the Careers Service, which is run by Local Education Authorities; careers teachers and other teachers in schools and colleges of further education; careers services in universities, polytechnics and colleges of higher education; Educational Guidance Services for Adults; and private careers guidance consultancies. Careers guidance elements enter into the roles of the staff of Jobcentres and Employment Offices and also into the work of Training Agents in Employment Training. In addition, employers often provide guidance to their own employees: while much of this is informal, some is 'formal' either as a specialised activity within the organisation or on a subcontracted basis.

C. Complications

We have said that we are reluctant to impose arbitrary limits upon our definition of careers guidance. Notwithstanding this, the evidence reviewed in Section Three concerns the effectiveness of 'formal' guidance as offered by public bodies to the general public, or by private organisations to a more limited clientele, or by educational and employing institutions to their own students or employees. It can scarcely be a matter for surprise that 'informal' guidance – the type provided most notably by family and friends – has not been evaluated. But in a sense, all of the evidence about the effects of guidance relates indirectly to informal channels. They exist, and their effects contribute to the background hum against which formal provision must make its voice heard. In controlled trials, for example, 'no guidance' (by which is meant no *formal* guidance) control subjects remain exposed to informal sources. In the longer term, informal guidance may contribute, to an unknown degree, to any erosion of the visible advantages of those receiving formal guidance. Our analysis of the economic potential of guidance in Section Two similarly takes 'informal' provision as a given.

But there have been several more difficult decisions to take about what we should or should not include within the scope of this review. Placement is one such difficult area. The term can signify that an individual succeeds in obtaining a position notified to him or her by a guidance agency, but it can also mean that the guidance agency is more actively involved in facilitating the process of application, arranging appointments and so on. This can be accompanied by 'advocacy', which is, as its name implies, the attempt to persuade recruiters (or education and training providers) on the individual's behalf. Placement is likely to be associated with guidance (as we have defined it) to some degree, in the sense that it is likely to be associated with the transmission of option information, the consideration of alternatives, and hence decision making. But another way of putting this is that much of what is called 'placement' does *not* fall within the scope of our definition. We shall accordingly refer only briefly to the effects of placement by agencies which also offer guidance.

Another complication arises because guidance has increasingly come to be seen by its practitioners as facilitating *learning*. This is quite consistent with the position we have taken. But one of the categories of learning routinely taken as a goal does not rest easily with our definition. The difficulties are similar to those already discussed with regard to 'placement'. The category of learning in question is called 'transition skills', by which is generally meant the skill of self-directed option search, but also those of application, self-advocacy and, sometimes, of managing or coping with the transition into new positions once obtained. In addition, recent important developments in guidance practice have emphasised the role of *social support*, particularly that available in group guidance activities, and particularly during job search. Thus it is often not possible on the evidence to distinguish the effects of guidance as we have so far defined it, from the effects of guidance more broadly defined. Instruction in at least part of 'transition skills', and social support in job search, are particularly important cases in point. It would seriously hinder the work of review in Section Three if studies of the effects of guidance which include these elements were set aside, and we have not attempted to do so.

This takes us on to an important general point. It is possible, and from the point of view of economic analysis fundamentally necessary, to make precise and limited definitions. In their absence, one simply cannot think through the issues. But when we return to the 'real world', we repeatedly find that two conditions apply. First, guidance interventions are more comprehensive in scope than can be contained in our definition. Second, guidance interventions are themselves part of activities (such as training programmes) which are broader than any of the current views of guidance to which we have referred.

The chief art of evaluation research is to find ways of disentangling the effects of what concerns one (here, guidance as we define it) from the effects of the totality in which it is embedded. Investigators have sometimes done relevant work even though it has not been precisely focused upon guidance. But, as we shall see, there are cases in which to separate guidance, or particular elements of it, from a totality is akin to removing a vital cog from a machine. If one did this, one would expect neither the cog, nor the remainder of the machine, to produce anything.

D. Who Benefits?

There is an opposition within the literature of guidance between those who see it as being wholly centred upon the individual, and those who see it as having to preserve a balance between individual benefit and social benefit. The fact that we started by stressing individual choice, and then proposed that guidance only qualifies as such when it is devised to help individuals, might be thought to put us in the camp of the individualists. But this is not necessarily so. One may offer individualised help with the underlying aim of contributing towards a better, happier or more productive society. The individual focus of guidance seems to be inherent to the type of activity which it is, but one may still provide this individual help with wider economic and social objectives in view. Indeed, one of the questions which our review of public benefits must consider is how far an individually focused service can provide wider benefits. Another question to be considered is whether a different approach — for example, focusing upon institutional reform rather than individual services — would be likely to be more effective in wider economic terms.

In point of fact, we shall be concerned with both the costs and benefits of guidance to three sets of actors:
(i) The individuals to whom guidance is offered, and who may or may not bear the cost.
(ii) Institutions: chiefly employers, but also educational institutions.
(iii) The public, by which we mean the general or collective good, or the costs and benefits of guidance as they impinge on the conditions of life of the average member of the general public, irrespective of whether he or she, as an individual (i) or an employer (ii), is a *direct* beneficiary.

E. Economic Effects

The following sections have quite different jobs to do and in consequence are written in different ways. Section Three is a review of research, and reflects the preoccupations of those who have conducted that research. For the most part, these have been psychologists and guidance practitioners, in education and elsewhere. They have sometimes had 'economic benefits' in mind, but have seldom approached them as an economist might do. The outcomes they have actually measured are, therefore, often intervening or mediating variables which are *presumed to imply* economic benefits. Two common examples are duration of job search and frequency of job changing. It is often plausibly assumed that by minimising these things, guidance leads to economic advantages both for individuals and their employers. This is because they are taken to denote lowered job-search and employee-search costs, successful and productive placement, diminished training costs, etc.

Plausible as these assumptions may be, they are only assumptions. From the individual point of view, entry into an occupation at a wage level below that of welfare payment would yield a negative economic return. In our second example, rapid job changing might imply that individuals enjoyed rapid salary increase or the benefits of intentional temporary employment. Employers might benefit from flexibility and the opportunity to screen recruits on-the-job.

These studies, therefore, do not provide a complete economic analysis of the cases they examine. But they can be interpreted in such a way that they provide a part of the economic picture. And in fact, when one looks at other areas of research where economic methods have been more directly applied, a partial or selective analysis is usually the most that has been achieved. Re-interpreting the evaluation research on the effects of guidance does not diminish it, but tends to reveal additional possibilities in what has been done and in what might be done.

Section Two of this review will discuss the potential effects of guidance from the viewpoint of the labour market. It will do so in part by considering guidance within the framework supplied by some 'economic models' of the workings of the labour market, although it will also look less formally at some recent institutional developments. It may be helpful to prepare the ground for Section Two by clarifying some of the main notions drawn from economics, which will be brought into play there. At the same time, this preliminary discussion, following upon our attempt to define the nature and scope of guidance itself, will help to show how Section Two of the report relates to Section Three, where existing research on the effects of guidance is reviewed.

Popularly, economics is assumed to be 'about money'. But at a more fundamental level, economics is 'about utility'. As the practitioners of guidance are well-aware, job-seekers consider much more than the pay on offer. They may regard the ability of a job to satisfy their interests and the conditions of work as important too. Indeed, these features of occupational decision-making are repeated objects of investigation. Economists also view the utility of a job (to the individual) as subjective and dependent upon the weights attached to such elements. There is, then, no fundamental opposition between an economic outlook and the outlook of guidance professionals.

But anyone involved with the practical application of the tools of economic analysis does, in reality, work with financial measures. Economic analysis relies upon money as the measure of many things which otherwise would be difficult or, practically speaking, impossible to measure. Of course, some things do get left out as one confines one's attention to financial measures and financial relationships. Provided that one does not ignore these, then much can still be gained by developing an analysis of financial and measurable aspects to the fullest possible degree. This is a worthwhile mental discipline in its own right.

In Section Two, the review of guidance will largely be in financial terms. As has already been made clear, this does not claim to be the whole of the story, and certainly it leaves out many qualitative and hard-to-measure elements required for a complete picture. But, as the financial aspects have not in the past received the attention they deserve, giving them some attention will help to develop a balanced view.

In order to assess the potential effects of guidance, we will try to show how it fits into a number of 'economic models' of labour-market processes. For example, the process of looking for a job is analysed by 'models of job search'. Economists present these models in terms of mathematical functions or equations, but in Section Two the presentation will be confined to fairly simple models which can be outlined, rather informally, in words. Models, whether mathematical or conceptual, are widely used by all kinds of social scientists – for example, by psychologists and sociologists as well as by economists. The criticism which is often directed at economic models, and those of other disciplines, is that they are over-simple and do scant justice to reality. In the case of economic models, this is often connected to the point that they are confined to financially measurable elements and leave out the 'softer' aspects, a point which has just been discussed. The more general issue of simplified models, and how to use them, is however worth an extra comment.

The chief point to make is that how far one should simplify reality is a practical matter. If the model helps one to see aspects which would otherwise be hidden, and to clarify the issues involved in policy decisions, then it is a useful model. If it obfuscates, then it is not. This is one of the strongest arguments, in fact, for keeping the models simple. Simple models must of course bring out some aspects of reality, and their limitations should be clearly understood. Provided that these conditions are met, then they can be helpful in at least three ways:

(i) They make assumptions explicit. This in turn stimulates thinking about assumptions, which is often a valuable exercise.
(ii) They provide a framework in which it is easier to think through the repercussions of changes (or answer 'what if ...?' questions).
(iii) The gap between the model and reality often helps to define the nature of the problem being analysed. For example, economic models generally

assume that people make choices in a rational way, and then go on to specify how rational choices would operate. Then we can see more clearly where, in reality, the obstacles to this kind of rational choice occur.

On balance, we believe that the simple conceptual models of labour-market processes which we use in Section Two are helpful to a consideration of the effects of guidance. If others find them helpful, that will be the justification for using them, even though they leave out much that is of interest.

Some of the most basic concepts used in the labour-market models are worth noting, and briefly remarking upon, at this point. The labour market itself is one of those concepts. The notion is that people offer their labour and that employers seek labour, both as free agents and for their own interests. Conventionally, individuals or workers are referred to as the supply side (because they supply labour), while employers are referred to as the demand side (because they look for labour). The filling of a job is, either implicitly or explicitly, the result of a bargain based on, or at least involving, prices. This gives rise to competition to get jobs. It is this competition which regulates, or rationalises, the prices of labour (that is, wages); conversely, wages reflect the state of competition or the balance between supply and demand. Competition however is not necessarily perfect, and wages may reflect other things than the state of competition for jobs.

Much interest has been directed, in recent years, to the notion of 'market failure', and in Section Two we will be discussing some problems and costs resulting from market failures. There can be various types of market failure, but one of the most important, and most relevant for present purposes, is connected with the notion of 'market signals'. Prices, and changes in prices, are assumed to be one of the main ways in which the state of the market is communicated to employers, workers, or other economic actors. If prices are not responsive to changes in the conditions of the market, it is hard for people to know what is going on. For example, if a certain kind of job is becoming obsolete, but firms are continuing to offer high wages, people may be misled into taking courses to become qualified for the job in question. Or the reverse might happen, with wages failing to rise in 'skill shortage' areas, so that workers do not come forward to fill the opportunities.

Differences between short-term signals and long-term outcomes, or general lack of signals relating to the long-term, may also contribute to market failures. People may tend to act upon a narrow range of information, mostly about the short-term, when rational decisions require a longer-term view. It is accordingly sometimes argued that the public authorities have a role in making good the deficiency. Whether intended as market signals or not, increases or decreases in subject places at universities, or public plans to encourage certain kinds of training, probably do influence people's views of the future. More generally, people can be influenced by informed advice.

An important concept in the analysis of labour markets, and one which will be used a great deal in Section Two of this report, is 'information'. It is important to appreciate that in economic analysis this word is used *in a very wide sense*. A guidance professional might think of information as but one aspect, even a minor aspect, of guidance, but an economist might think of guidance as but one aspect of information. In this latter sense, information is any kind of input to a decision or choice. Reading job advertisements in the local paper, and having a careers counselling session, would both be inputs to the process of finding a job, and so both would qualify as information. And, of course, the information (in the ordinary sense) passed on within a guidance or counselling session also counts as information (in the economic sense). Again, the gains in self-awareness, or in understanding of how to evaluate alternatives, which may be part of the results of guidance, can also be considered as part of the broad economic concept of 'information'.

Closely allied, and equally broad, is the notion of 'information costs'. From an economic viewpoint, information is never entirely free of cost, because at the very least it takes some time to acquire, and time is a most important resource. In fact, there is much to be said (in an economic analysis) for considering information entirely in terms of information costs. Just as information can be though of as any input to a decision, so it can also be thought of as what it costs to arrive at a decision.

F. A Distinction

Most of us are familiar with the idea that guidance is associated with *transitions*. Guidance thus deals with movement across boundaries, both abstract (as between employment statuses) and organisational. Increasingly, however, systems are being devised to which guidance is integral. Of course, this guidance often concerns decision points and to this extent is associated with transitions, but the crucial factor is that guidance is perceived to have a *system management* role. In effect, it is assumed that in order for a new set of institutional arrangements to 'work', guidance must be built into them. This occurs quite widely, both in the development of complex educational systems (e.g. the credit accumulation and transfer system) and in the pursuit of flexibility and other human resource objectives in complex internal labour markets. In Section Three, we shall briefly note the existence of evaluation studies which have somewhat artificially attempted to disentangle the 'effects' of guidance from those of the training and rehabilitation programmes of which it forms an integral part.

In Section Two, under the headings of 'processes' and 'problems', we discuss the traditional economic approach to guidance, which sees it essentially as a method for addressing market imperfections. These imperfections have usually been seen to affect movement into and out of the labour market, and the directions of movements between employers, occupations and VET options: which is to say, 'transitions'. Thereafter, under the heading of 'new institutions' we discuss the place of guidance in institutional change.

G. Overview

In the pages which follow we look at what can be called 'formal' guidance. The sorts of activities covered by this term include careers education in schools, the work of the Careers Service and other providers, and special initiatives for adult job seekers. Without descending into the fine details of definition, it should be plain that we mean the kinds of guidance of concern to policy makers. We use the terms 'careers guidance' and (more briefly) 'guidance' to refer to the help which is given to individuals to acquire, organise and use a wide range of information (including information about themselves), to think-through issues and to take decisions about their employment, education and training. We recognise that guidance can go wider than this. In our review of evidence we shall make one or two very limited concessions to the wider view, but our chief focus of concern should be plain.

We proceed in three steps. In Section Two, we ask what economic models of the labour market can tell us about the economic potential of guidance. By this we mean economic benefits to individuals, employers and educational institutions and the nation as a whole. We also look very briefly at the potential guidance has as an instrument of institutional change. In Section Three we review the research evidence as it currently stands. The novelty of this section lies less in the studies it has collected together than in the way in which those studies have been scrutinised. For the first time this has been done against a reasonably considered view of economic potential. We reveal a variety of encouraging findings, but also point to a number of gaps in our current knowledge. We make no apology for adopting a rather tough stance with regard to the quality of evidence, since at the end of the day this allows us to be reasonably confident about what we do and do not know.

Finally, in Section Four, we outline our view of what guidance evaluation should look like in the future. We believe that the gaps to which we have alluded should be filled, and that the difficulties experience by evaluators in the past offer some important pointers to the way in which research should be conducted in the future. But we also believe that if we are to move away from counting processes and towards assessing outcomes it will be necessary to embed evaluation against outcomes much more firmly into the practice of guidance. This implies a 'culture of evaluation' in which guidance agencies and practitioners are participants, rather than the objects of occasional external scrutiny. This implies, in turn, that they should be provided with the tools and encouragement they will need for this purpose.

Section Two: The Potential for Guidance: Ideas from Economics
Michael White

In this section, we consider how careers guidance might make a difference to the workings of the labour market, and so seek an indication of what its economic value might be.

The discussion in this section is conceptual and exploratory, and offers no hard-and-fast demonstrations or prescriptions. Nor can we claim to offer a sophisticated analysis. To a large extent, we are beginning from the beginning. This is because until now, as explained in Section One, little effort has been devoted to analysing guidance in specifically economic terms, although as explained in Section Three, relevant information has sometimes been collected. This lack of explicit economic evaluation partly reflects the ways in which the providers and practitioners of guidance have seen its role. Another reason is the disciplinary gap between professionals in the guidance field on one hand and economists and researchers on the other. A goal here is to find common ground between the concepts of guidance and the concepts of labour market analysis. It is also worth saying that, even if guidance practice has not been explicitly directed towards economic ends, it could already be serving them quite well. We have to remember the man who was unaware that he had been writing prose!

The discussion will consider the potential effects of guidance at three levels. The first level is rather abstract and relates to broad labour market processes; the aim is to see how guidance would fit into these. The second level is more concrete, consisting of some important problems of the labour market; by indicating the costs imposed by these problems, we can also get some feel of the potential cost savings if better guidance could help to reduce the problems. Finally, the assessment is completed by considering some institutional developments in the labour market, and asking what guidance could be expected to contribute to the success of these developments.

A. Labour Market Decisions
Three main kinds of decision or choice are generally referred to in economic analyses of the labour market. These are:
a) Decisions about whether to offer one's labour, and if so for how many hours of work
b) Decisions about how much education and training to invest in (or of which sorts)
c) Decisions about which jobs to apply for or accept.

These three types of decisions are often referred to, respectively, as labour supply, human capital, and job search.

Guidance (in the sense outlined in Section One) is mainly given to individuals. Accordingly, the focus here is on decisions made by individuals, the suppliers of labour. The other side of the labour market, the demand for labour created by employers, will largely be left out of the analysis, although it would certainly be of interest to consider the possible role of labour market advisory services offered to employers.

Guidance is more obviously relevant to decisions of types (b) and (c), in the list above, than for the general labour supply decision (a). Nevertheless, it is useful to begin with (a), because it is the most basic labour market decision. It is also a useful start to consider how this labour market decision is formulated in economic terms.

a) *Labour Supply Decisions*
In any text-book of economics, one of the basic notions put forward is the 'labour supply curve'. This depicts working (for money) essentially as a trade-off. It shows that people choose the amount of time they give to paid work in such a way as to balance income against what is usually called, perhaps unhelpfully, 'leisure' (it might be better thought of as domestic, non-waged production). If working (more) is likely to provide substantially higher income, then an individual will be more willing to take on the work, than if it offers only a small increase in income.

Of course, this is a simplistic, and largely unreal, model of behaviour (for further details and criticism, a useful text is that by Joll, McKenna, McNabb and Shorey, 1983). In real life, individual decisions about labour supply are set in a framework of family roles and budgets, and fairly rigid employer policies. Most men and single women are expected, and expect, to supply their labour on a full-time basis for paid work. The groups where real decisions exist are those at the fringes of the labour force: students, lone parents, women who have left work to have children, people approaching or at retirement age. Surveys in a number of countries have shown that there are large proportions of workers who would like to work fewer hours but do not have the opportunity (see, for example, Best, 1980; Koller, Reyher and Teriet, 1982). At the same time, many people who would like to work, either full-time or part-time, are unable to get a job. And there are many employers with vacancies that they cannot fill for substantial periods. These are all indications of market imperfections: the market is not working sufficiently well to permit supply and demand decisions to be in balance.

The way in which labour supply is imagined to work (in economic theory), and the way it actually works, pose several issues for guidance services. The basic labour supply model assumes that the workers are perfectly informed about wages. It is wages, or more generally prices, which do the work of communication in much of economic theory. But, of course, information about wages has to come from somewhere. The existence of market imperfections might suggest that wage information is lacking to some of the participants in the market: not knowing the financial opportunities they are missing, they fail to put themselves forward. So it would seem reasonable to suppose that one of the functions of guidance could be to provide information about wages. This is perhaps not how guidance professionals see their role, even if they bear in mind the extremely broad definition of 'information' which applies in economics (see Section One, page 9). Yet, while not giving specific information about wages in this or that job (perhaps more the role of the placement service), guidance may be able to provide people with a 'feel' for market opportunities. For example, they may point out which are the 'better jobs' (for people of given qualifications, etc.), or tell people about opportunities of which they were previously ignorant. In either case the individuals concerned may then follow up by finding out more specific details. Seen in this way, the provision of 'economic' information is perhaps not so far from the established guidance notions of 'learning outcomes' which are discussed in Section One and in Section Three.

The basic labour supply model, as it assumes information to be available, pays no attention to how information is provided or delivered. In effect, it assumes the technology or infrastructure of information to be fixed. Guidance can be seen as part of this infrastructure. What happens if guidance systems are improved so that individuals get, on average, better information about employment opportunities, and better information about their own skills or worth, than they had previously? On balance it seems unlikely that this will discourage many people from offering their labour. More probably, the increased information would stimulate labour supply and hence competition in the job market. Wages would tend to be reduced as the labour supply rose. Lower wages would then stimulate employers to produce more goods and services, and this would increase their need for labour. This in turn would raise wages. A new balance would be struck between supply and demand. This would result in more employment than at the start.

Of course, this is only a notional argument. It would have to be a powerful form of guidance to have an appreciable effect upon the labour supply, especially as the existing labour market infrastructure is quite extensive. Both public job services and private employment bureaux are offering information about job availability, hours of work, and wages, to people such as women returners and students who have a critical need for such information in making their supply decisions. If these information services were not available, employers would find it more difficult to find new sources of labour supply and economic growth would be inhibited. Guidance professionals may think of their role as highly distinct from that of the placement services, but from an economic viewpoint the functions are similar in this case: both are facilitating supply by expanding individuals' awareness of opportunities. Perhaps guidance services should give more consideration to the roles they could develop in this respect, for example by helping women returners, retired people and others to find their way back into the job market.

b) Human Capital Decisions

According to the human capital theory of neoclassical economics, an individual invests in education and training in order to reap long-term returns (the classical exposition is that of Becker, 1975; there is a useful introduction in Joll and colleagues, 1983). By speaking of education and training as an investment, this theory draws attention, in the first place, to the costs which anyone incurs who devotes effort to education and training. These include the costs of foregone wages or household production (including 'leisure'), and the direct costs of fees, books, and so so. The need to consider the returns to education and training arise from a recognition of these costs. In some cases, the returns are intrinsic, and education and training are then spoken of as a consumption good. However, in many cases qualifications open the way to better-paid and more interesting or pleasant jobs or careers, and it is reasonable to suppose that it is these likely returns which frequently motivate education and training.

The theory goes further, in predicting that each individual will continue to invest in education and training so long as this brings her/him future returns which, properly discounted, are greater than the costs of the investment. Conversely, a person is presumed to stop education and training when the costs becomes too high relative to the expected returns. At the extreme, if a person were to try to get a qualification which was beyond his/her capacity, the costs would tend towards infinity (as the course would never be completed), and the expected returns would be negative.

On the employers' side, the payment of higher wages is supposed to reflect productivity. Accordingly, the value of education and training lies in its contribution to productivity, which is reflected in wages. A virtuous circle is completed, in which employers pay more for the education and training completed, provided that this yields higher productivity, while individuals pursue more education and training so long as it yields higher wages.

This is highly idealized. The wages received by individuals are influenced by factors other than their skills and experience, such as gender, trade union policies, or rigidity on the part of employers. In addition, sociologists have shown through detailed research that there are powerful subjective biasses in educational and training choices (see, for example, the review by Smith, 1978; or Breen, 1984). Many people seem to be unaware of the opportunities for higher earnings through qualifications, or if aware, to disregard them because the pay-off is too distant. In families with small resources, the costs of education and training are frequently seen as prohibitive (Halsey, Heath and Ridge, 1980; Gambetta, 1987). Although it is less often remarked upon, there is also good evidence that some young people are pushed by their parents to pursue educational goals which are too difficult for them (ibid.), and this, if considered as an investment, may produce poor returns.

To a large extent, then, human capital theory explains why qualifications do pay off, but fails to predict under-investment and over-investment in education and training by many people. This offers a natural opportunity for the provision of improved guidance, and it is of course one recognized by the guidance professions.

The information required by individuals to make fully rational decisions, of the type envisaged by economic theory, about education and training is enormous, and the impossibility of achieving such a level of knowledge provides a partial explanation of under-investment. In principle, the individual should be able to foresee all the occupations which a particular kind of qualification will lead into, and should also be able to compare this with similar information for all other available qualifications. People not only lack this kind of systematic information, they may also be unaware of whole large sections of the map. For example, some young people may know only about those parts of the occupational map which members of their family have worked in, and may have erroneous notions about the returns from other occupations with different qualification requirements. So one of the straightforward benefits of guidance will be 'mapping' to make more people aware of the occupational possibilities and potential returns from different types of qualification. To the extent that this leads to reduced under-investment in education and training, there would be benefits both to individuals (higher incomes) and to the economy (higher productivity).

It should be appreciated, moreover, that because of the sheer volume of detail and complexity involved in human capital decisions, people are unlikely to be helped much by simply being given large masses of raw data. Help with structuring the choices and selecting the information which is relevant would be far more useful. A psychologist might describe this in terms of learning strategies or information integration. An economist would tend to see the distinction in terms of information costs. The undigested data would be useless precisely because of the immense time (and hence cost) which would be involved in the process of sorting and assimilation. The higher-level approach offered by skilled guidance permits the individual to develop a relevant map of the decision in an affordable time.

Finally, a subtler impact of improved guidance in this area could be in terms of assurance or risk reduction. When people are making decisions, it is not only the expected outcome which may weigh with them, but also the uncertainty or variability of that outcome. Those who have the least resources are also likely to have the lowest tolerance of financial risk. If guidance can increase confidence in the feasibility of outcomes (such as achieving a certain level of qualification) then decisions will be shifted in that direction. Similarly, there will be savings for those who are deterred from taking a course which does not fit their capabilities. Of course, such gains from guidance are only possible if guidance is, in fact, sufficiently accurate and reliable.

c) *Job Search Decisions*

Job search is a process which people must go through when they do not have a job and want one, or when they have a job which is no longer satisfactory to them and they want to move. Job search theory sets up models of how people negotiate this process and make choices among the potentially

The Economic Value of Careers Guidance

wide range of search paths open to them (again, the text by Joll and colleagues, 1983, provides a suitable introduction to this topic). Job search would appear to be a particularly attractive framework in which to evaluate the potential economic benefits of guidance, because an explicit part of even the simplest models of job search consists of the costs of acquiring information about jobs, and especially about the wages attached to jobs. At the same time, consideration of job search leads to some crucial questions about the relation between information, information costs, and guidance.

There are numerous competing models of job search. A fairly simple one assumes that individuals make an application for, or accept an employer's offer for, any relevant job which provides rewards at or above some threshold, usually referred to as the reservation wage (not all job search models make use of a reservation wage concept, but this is the dominant approach). The need for individuals to have a reservation wage arises because of uncertainty (incomplete information) about the wage offers which exist in the labour market.

The level of the reservation wage is crucial for job search behaviour and hence for the economics of the labour market. Job-seekers with relatively high reservation wages are (if rational, and genuinely seeking employment) committed to relatively large amounts of search. This follows from the consideration that, the higher the reservation wage, the fewer the jobs which will satisfy the condition, and the harder they will be to find. Conversely, those with rather low reservation wages will (rationally) engage in relatively small amounts of job search. This is because, in the first place, a large proportion of available jobs will satisfy the reservation wage (almost any job will do); and in the second place (more important for the purposes of this paper), job search costs will loom larger relative to (low) expected wages. A person with a low reservation wage may be quite rational in keeping job search barely ticking over while waiting for something to turn up.

One unreality in this model is that all job-seekers are assumed to be capable of doing any jobs. A more realistic job search model begins by recognizing that each person screens out, or simply does not observe, a large proportion of all vacancies (for an example of this approach, see Narendranathan and Nickell, 1989). Carpenters do not look at advertisements in accountancy magazines, and accountants do not look for jobs in the trade press of the construction industry. So each type of person, depending on such characteristics as qualifications and experience, faces a different job search problem, based on a particular wage distribution for those jobs which are accessible, and the search costs for those kinds of jobs. This complicates the decision for the job-seeker, because he/she must judge the area of search as well as fixing a reservation wage.

One further complication is worth bringing into the picture, for our purposes. This is the time dimension. Searching for a job not only imposes information costs, it also takes time. Suppose that the job-seeker is either unemployed or underpaid relative to his/her market value. Then the quicker a job (above the current income level) is found, the sooner does increased income begin to flow in, while the longer that he/she continues to search, the greater the potential earnings foregone. Of course, these short-term gains or losses have to be set against the potential longer-term considerations of getting a still better paid job by continuing the search for longer. What job search theory predicts is that, faced with these time-related costs, individuals will progressively adjust their reservation wages downward, the longer that they search without success. To start with they try to maximize their expected returns in the long run, but later this is outweighed by the rising time-related costs of search: they 'cut their losses'. However, as reservation wages fall, so too (in accordance with the earlier part of the discussion) does job search decrease.

Having outlined some of the main economic ideas concerning job search, we can now consider how the provision of guidance could be expected to influence job-seeking behaviour. The most obvious effect would be in terms of reducing the cost of information. Suppose that information about jobs and wages can only be obtained by visiting employers' premises and making inquiries there: job search will then be costly, especially as many of these visits may prove to be wasted. But if a service is able to supply updates about a wide range of potential vacancies, and to transmit market signals about the distribution of wages likely to be found, then search costs will be considerably reduced. The effects of this, if economic theories are on the right lines, will be to increase the amount of job search, for a given reservation wage, by comparison with the hypothetical case where no such service exists. Moreover, because people would be able to search through more vacancies for a given cost, their reservation wages would tend to rise (they could afford to be more ambitious).

This would have important consequences for individuals, employers, and the labour market. The most positive effect would be that individuals would tend to be better allocated to jobs because of the increased search, and this should also result in higher average productivity. In other words, there would be fewer cases in which individuals took jobs which were much below their abilities (an inevitable consequence of imperfect information and limited search). The effects upon wages are less easy to assess a priori. If the service was available only to a limited number of job-seekers, then these should obtain higher average wages than if they were without the service. Their information costs would be lower than that of competitors, so their reservation wage would be closer to the optimum and their search more efficient. But if all job-seekers received the same service, the effect on actual wages would be indeterminate, because while reservation wages would initially rise, this would later be offset by the greater competition for jobs resulting from higher general intensities of job search.

Of course, this example is not so much about the potential for improvement as the hypothetical costs of being without existing services. There already exist job advertisements in local papers, and placement services offering a wide range of information about specific job opportunities. The costs of search may be quite low already in terms of getting information of this relatively simple type, but there may be relatively high costs in terms of making job applications and travelling to attend job interviews. To improve on the existing information services may be rather difficult, because of the sheer size, complexity, and changeability of the job market. Indeed, if methods of improving job information substantially were feasible, they would surely be developed commercially, since job-seekers would benefit greatly from them. In practice, one observes commercial job agencies which sell their services to employers, not to job-seekers; this suggests that the kind of advantageous and low-cost information needed by individuals is difficult to provide.

However, there are other possibilities. Guidance (rather than just job information) could influence job search by helping people to assess their own potential and so establish their reservation wage in a realistic way. Economic models of job search do not seem to accord with what is known about the ways in which reservation wages are actually set (although research on the latter is rather limited). For example, many people (even in unemployment) seem simply to take their previous wage, or the wage which they regard as being necessary to provide a certain standard of living for their family (see White and McRae, 1989; McLoughlin, Millar and Cooke, 1989). These may be inappropriate if, in fact, jobs at this level of pay are not available in current circumstances. Further, there is evidence to show that many unemployed people accept actual job offers below their reservation wage, which indicates that their reservation wages are rather weakly formulated in the first place (White and McRae, 1989). Economic models tend to ignore individuals' knowledge of their own market value, but this is surely as relevant to the setting of a reservation wage as knowledge of the market. In general, by having unrealistically high reservation wages, individuals will engage in a great deal of search with little chance of success; by having unduly low reservation wages, individuals will be demotivated to seek for jobs, or may end up in jobs well below their capacities (with consequent productivity losses for the economy). Guidance which helped people to form a clearer view of these issues should lead to better job search strategies and more satisfactory outcomes.

A further contribution from guidance would concern the definition of the segments of job opportunities which would be worth investigating, for that individual. This part of the decision process may be particularly crucial for unemployed people who have to consider occupational mobility as one of their options. If an individual defines the job segment to be searched in too narrow a way, then there is a danger of not being able to find sufficient vacancies. If, on the other hand, attention is spread over too wide a range of jobs, then search may be ineffective (for example, excess costs may be incurred, and potential employers may form the view that the person 'doesn't know his/her own mind'). Here, if the necessary knowledge were available to guidance specialists (such as the skills common to various occupations, or the willingness of employers in one branch to consider as relevant the experience gained in another type of industry), this could be of special value to job-seekers.

One further form of help in job search may be to remove or weaken 'self-discrimination' constraints which are limiting the chances of individuals. People must narrow down their span of attention when looking for jobs, but in doing so they may exclude real opportunities. For example, there is some evidence to suggest that members of ethnic minorities or those with substantial periods of unemployment may exclude themselves from white-collar jobs, when employers would actually welcome their applications (Crowley-Bainton and White, 1990). Older workers may regard their chances of finding re-employment as much lower than is actually the case (Jolly, Creigh and Mingay, 1980). Advice which removes or weakens such constraints will once again tend to raise reservation wages and stimulate more extensive job search.

In conclusion, the support of job search decisions should provide as fruitful an area for the application of guidance services (over and above existing job-data provision through placement agencies) as educational or vocational choice. The most obvious type of service, namely to reduce the information costs of job search, may be difficult to achieve in practice, although even marginal technical improvements should be worth having (provided that they reduce public as well as private costs of information). Where guidance (rather than mere information provision) should have most scope to improve the effectiveness of job search, is in the more 'qualitative' aspects which are least well analysed in the relatively simplistic job search models of economic theory. The value of job search theory in assessing the role of guidance lies not only in suggesting why this support is needed, but also in indicating the kinds of benefit which are likely to arise. These could be described as 'better targeted' job search strategies leading to improved allocation of people to jobs.

B. Guidance and Problems of the Labour Market

The gist of the preceding section was that the efficient working of the labour market, as conceived in a number of economic theories, assumes that individuals make well informed choices, but that this is not in practice always the case. Common observation or the findings of research tends to show that deficiencies of information, or as psychologists might also say, difficulties of information integration, set limits to the efficiency of the labour market. It would be wrong to attribute all the failings of labour markets to problems of information, and it is important to keep a sense of proportion. But specific problems of improperly informed choices make a natural focus for a consideration of the potential contribution of guidance. We shall focus on three problems, all of which offer some scope for quantification.

a) Drop-Outs From Education and Training

Although there have been steady gains in the rates of basic-level qualification in the UK, there remains a substantial proportion of young people who leave school without a qualification of any sort (this even applies in Scotland, with its relatively high average level of qualification). In addition, there are others who obtain only a nominal level of qualification which does not even guarantee that they are functionally literate or numerate. Depending upon the stringency of the criterion which is applied, it would appear that between 10 and 30 per cent of school leavers in the UK could be regarded as under-qualified for entrance to the labour market. On the basis of a recent review of the evidence, which took account also of a cross-national comparison, a figure of around 20 per cent would appear reasonable (see Hannan, Hovels, van den Berg and White, 1991). Subsequently, the members of this group tend to move into 'careers' consisting of shortlived, low-skilled jobs providing little or no training, and spells of unemployment.

The Potential for Guidance: Ideas from Economics

If they do participate in YTS/YT, they are highly likely to be found in the schemes offering less training, and they are also relatively unlikely to complete training and obtain qualifications (ibid. for sources).

Human capital theory, as discussed in Part A, can be applied to account for the existence of this group. Some part of it results from lack of capacity to learn and acquire skills. However, it seems unlikely that this could account for more than five per cent of the population. In Germany, for example, 92 per cent of school leavers have at least passed the Hauptschulabschluss, which consists of 9-10 subjects at lower GCSE grades (Rose and Wignanek, 1990). Equally high pass rates at basic level are achieved in a number of other countries, e.g. Japan. A study in the Netherlands identified only four per cent of school age children as lacking capacity to complete basic educational qualifications (Hannan and colleagues, 1991). It seems reasonable to infer that low levels of attainment in the UK reflect individual choices (which, of course, are likely to be conditioned by economic and social circumstances) for at least 15 per cent of the age group. That is, the young people concerned could get better qualifications, but see no advantage in devoting effort to their education and training (this is shown variously by low attendance, by not taking examinations, and by not entering, or not completing, later training courses). Is this a form of market failure?

The market could fail in two rather different ways. First, it might be disadvantageous for the individual to make these negative educational choices, but there might be a failure of information (that is, the individual makes the choice under misinformation). Alternatively, the individual's decision may be rational in personal terms, but may result in public if not personal costs; here the market is wrongly structured with respect to qualifications (or vice versa), with rewards to individuals who have acquired skills (or not) out of proportion to the productive value of skills to the national economy.

An analysis recently carried out as part of another study (see Hannan and colleagues, 1991) suggests that non-qualification results, in the UK, in relatively low financial losses to individuals (by comparison with gaining low levels of qualification), but in rather high public financial costs. This arises because (a) the average wage differentials between non-qualified persons and those with the lower levels of qualification are rather small, and indeed are in favour of the non-qualified group in the early years after entry to the labour market; and (b) there are substantial differences in unemployment rates between the two groups concerned, especially in the early years again, which result in heavy direct public costs. Non-qualification tends to be associated with early family formation and large family size; therefore benefit costs are high, and the gap between wages and benefits relatively small, for the non-qualified group.

A first estimate of the public costs to non-qualification can be made on the basis of the differential unemployment rates, multiplied by average differential benefit and social security costs, between the two groups. It can be seen from Box A that these costs are rather substantial. It might be argued, of course, that higher qualification rates among those presently nonqualified would not automatically lead to proportional increases in employment rates. Such an argument would particularly come from those who regard the demand for labour as independent of the labour supply. This now seems a questionable view, and one might well argue that increases in basic educational level would create more-than-proportional increases in employment rates, because of second-round effects on wage competition, and improvements in industrial productivity and competitiveness. Moreover, the calculation of Box A merely considers direct state expenditures. Better, from an economic viewpoint, would be to consider the foregone production resulting from unemployment, and this would be considerably greater than the direct exchequer cost.

Box A: Notional Exchequer costing of non-qualification

a) Restrict attention to under-30s (on the basis that qualification is less important later). It is estimated (roughly) that about 1.2 million under-30s lack useful labour market qualifications.

b) It is estimated that the unemployment rate among this group is about 13 percentage points greater than in the group with basic qualifications (4+ CSEs below grade 1). Deduct 5 percentage points from this to allow for those with learning difficulties etc. This leaves about 8 percentage points of 'excess unemployment' related to non-qualification.

c) Assume that the weekly benefit cost for an unemployed person aged under 30 is £70. Then the notional exchequer cost of non-qualification is 1.2m. x 0.08 x £70 x 52 or nearly £350 million per annum. (Lost tax revenue and lost production are ignored since they involve more extensive assumptions.)

d) Against this would have to be set any additional costs of raising qualification levels (but there is little evidence to suggest that increased expenditures have much to do with the issue). In addition, a more complete costing would have to take account of the further effects resulting from a raising of qualification levels. These could lead to a reduced estimate (via substitution, deadweight, etc.) or to an increased estimate (via stimulus to growth, competitiveness, etc.). The calculations are in any case rough and have made no allowance for the costs of Employment Training in unemployment, etc.

The Potential for Guidance: Ideas from Economics

We would maintain, therefore, that there is a potentially large payoff to be obtained from any form of guidance which made (or contributed towards) even a modest impact upon the problem of education and training drop-outs. The difficulty in attaining this at present, however, is the relatively small wage incentive for individuals – of the order of 10 per cent – between being non-qualified and having some relatively low qualifications. Taking into account opportunities in the informal economy, both before and after leaving school, one can see only too well why the lower levels of the opportunity structure of the UK labour market sustain and perpetuate these levels of non-qualification.

The potential for guidance could be considered under two scenarios: (a) intensified or innovative guidance within existing labour market structures, and (b) guidance in support of initiatives to reform labour market structures.

Table 2.1: Employment and wages of male 'early leavers' and other groups, aged 20–29, Great Britain, 1987

	Qualifications reported		
	None	*CSE*	*O-level*
Probability of employment	0.69	0.82	0.87
Median earnings in employment (£1987)	143.0	145.0	164.2

Sources: General Household Survey 1987; own supplementary calculations.

The notion of using guidance as a motivational force to help the existing labour market to work better may well run up against prevailing professional values in guidance. Given that the income differential between non-qualification and the adjacent level of qualification is so small, guidance policy could only make a difference if it were capable of supporting an ambitious raising of aspirations. Would this be asking guidance to assume too much of an interventionist role in the name of social welfare? The dilemma is posed by Table 2.1. While showing the poor returns to lower-level qualifications, this table also indicates much better returns to qualifications of the old O-level standard and above. If only one in 20 of current 'drop-outs' could be motivated to attain qualifications at this higher level, this would have substantial public (as well as personal) returns. This might be achievable if it were possible to identify, preferably inside the school system, those with substantial unrealised potential (under-achievers). Once it was possible to identify such individuals they could be provided with information and encouragement about the careers open to those with qualifications. This would have to be done sufficiently early to influence formative behaviour in school. However, the degree of selectivity and targeting implied might not be acceptable to many teachers and educationists as well as guidance professionals. Also, it is not clear whether guidance to raise aspiration levels would be effective without substantial changes in the surrounding systems of education.

There might be some scope for remedial guidance for those entering the labour market, or about to enter the labour market, although by this time many may have become committed to lowskilled work. The chances of breaking out of this trap would seem to depend largely, under existing labour market structures, on identifying abilities in individuals which they could develop through well-matched training or initial jobs. It seems likely that many non-qualified young people are screened out (or, equally, screen themselves out) before employers have the chance to assess their abilities or aptitudes. If guidance services and/or other arrangements with employers could lead to a more positive approach towards under-qualified young people, some fraction might be selected into 'second chance' training or job experience which would develop existing aptitudes. Similarly, the problem of young people with low educational levels tending to drop out of training (such as Youth Training) might be reduced if in-training guidance was more widely and more readily available. Once again, however, the feasibility of such an approach would depend on what guidance services are capable of achieving, and at what public cost.

But these suggestions could be dismissed as thinking too small. The basic problems appear to be the social circumstances which produce low aspiration levels and the labour market structures which then reinforce them and convert them into life strategies for the individuals concerned. If the labour market structures themselves change, in such a way as to counter the culture of low aspiration, then the possibility arises of more substantial improvements in qualification levels, and hence in employment prospects. Obviously, larger changes of this type could not be attributed to guidance, even if guidance formed a part of the reforms carried out. On the other hand, it is worth asking whether guidance is a necessary part of such reforms.

Reforms or innovations of direct relevance to the problem of 'drop-outs' are those described in the CBI report *Towards a Skills Revolution* (CBI, 1990), and the development of the training voucher idea advocated there. According to our analysis of the problem, young people without qualifications have in essence made a decision against education (perhaps by default) and existing arrangements in the labour market, with a fairly wide availability of low-skilled jobs for young people, create no pressure to revise this decision. The provision of training credits as an entitlement for labour market entrants creates, potentially, the need to give thought to training. As the CBI report stresses, it is difficult to see that this opportunity will be properly used unless guidance is provided at this choice point. This is likely to be particularly true of the group which we are focusing upon here. Since in the past they have 'opted out' of education, they will be least equipped to give it a fresh consideration. The family circumstances which may have influenced many of them to take a negative view of investment in their own future will also still be present, meaning that they have less possibility of turning in that direction for advice. In economic terms, the information costs of turning their training opportunity into a reality are too high, unless support is given. This is because they have not previously been giving much attention to the issue, and they do not have much access to relevant information in the ordinary course of life. They need guidance, but are unlikely to get it without a formalised provision of guidance services.

Proposed changes in the basic curriculum within schools are also worth considering at this point. The government proposal to extend the range of vocational subjects within the basic curriculum is germane. An argument against early choice of vocational subjects (and hence, the argument against a vocationalised curriculum) has been that such subjects are too narrow or specific, and may prove to have limited value if, subsequently, young people want to enter unrelated occupations. Once again, this is a problem of decision making under risk and with potentially high information costs if choices are to be rational rather than arbitrary. These considerations would seem to strengthen the case for vocational (as opposed to educational) guidance at about the same age, to be provided in a more intensive form than now. Guidance would then have the potential benefit of helping young people to choose subjects in such a way as to link up more directly with later training and jobs, as well as providing motivational signals about the jobs available to those who attain relevant qualifications. As always, we have to assume that guidance services would have the capacity to provide these linkages, although at present it may well be that they do not.

b) *Mismatch*

Mismatch is a notion used in guidance, usually referring to lack of fit between individuals' abilities and aspirations and the jobs which they obtain. The economic notion of mismatch is quite different, and refers to aggregate conditions in the labour market. Labour market mismatch can to some extent be seen as an extension and generalization of the particular problems represented by early drop-outs from education and training. The concept has been in currency for some years, but has remained rather vague. It has recently received a substantially new treatment (see Jackman, Layard and Savouri, 1990). Theirs is rather a difficult paper for non-specialists, and (in the present writers' view) does not provide a fully realistic account of the problem of mismatch. But it contains numerous ideas which we draw upon, and to which we add freely in a non-rigorous way. Among its achievements is to suggest how big the effect of mismatch may be, and hence (roughly and tentatively) to estimate its cost.

It is helpful to think of what a labour market without mismatch would be like. In such a labour market, rates of unemployment would be equal, or at least tending towards equality, between every significant sub-division of the labour force. Wherever one category of labour had excess unemployment, workers would be migrating out to other groups with lower unemployment, or wages in the high-unemployment group would be decreasing relative to other groups, to create greater cost-competitiveness for that category of labour and so reduce its unemployment. So a labour market without mismatch is characterized by homogeneity of unemployment, while a labour market with mismatch is characterized by heterogeneity or diversity of unemployment. Mismatch is, therefore, simply the accumulation of unemployment in certain pockets of the economy; or, at a deeper level, the processes which bring about this differentiation. The time dimension has to be brought into this, because mismatch is also the persistence of such differences over extended periods.

There are many respects in which unemployment rates differ between groups, and have done so for long periods. The outstanding example concerns the broad occupational levels of the labour force, with low unemployment among higher non-manual groups (the 'salariat' or 'service class'), and relatively much higher unemployment among manual workers (routine white collar workers occupy an intermediate position). This contrast might also be expressed in terms of education or qualification, which is highly correlated with occupation. There are substantial differences between industries, but much of this can be reduced to differences in composition by skill or occupational level between the industries. Other important dimensions of mismatch are gender, age group, and region.

An intuitively appealing picture of what is going on is that there are barriers between the various sections of the labour market, which make it difficult for unemployment to even itself out. For example, in the case of gender, women's jobs are highly segregated from men's, and are paid at lower wage rates (relative to human capital); so it is difficult and unattractive for unemployed men to move into the sections of the job market dominated by women. In the case of occupational differences, manual workers are less qualified than nonmanual workers, and have considerable difficulty in moving into the white-collar area except by the two narrow bridges of supervisory jobs and self-employment. Jackman and colleagues stress the importance of 'entry costs': for manual workers with low qualifications, the entry costs to white-collar jobs would arise from the need for substantial periods of training and, indeed, of remedial adult education. Moreover, because of barriers to inflow and outflow, the wage mechanisms of the labour market work imperfectly. Wages remain relatively high in parts of the labour market with low unemployment and low inflow rates, and the high level of wages in turn inhibits growth of demand for labour and hence sustains unemployment.

Jackman and colleagues assessed the contribution of all sources of mismatch to total unemployment at (roughly and tentatively) about one third. (They stress, quite rightly, that mismatch should not be thought of as a primary cause of unemployment; it can be thought of, rather, as a brake on the reduction of unemployment.) This figure of one third should not be taken too literally, but seems 'in the ball-park', if one also takes into account the other factors which are known to contribute to the overall problem. It would also not be unreasonable to suggest that occupational mismatch, by far the strongest factor, contributes one half of the mismatch effect. (Jackman and colleagues suggest a lower proportion, but do not seem to have taken into account the extent to which occupational differences enter into and underlie the other types of mismatch. We would argue that these differences are fundamental. For example, the unemployment problems of the 'drop-outs' discussed in the preceding section can be interpreted partly as mismatch between younger and older groups, but much better as mismatch between occupational groups among young people.)

With mismatch recognized as such a large component of unemployment, any measure which contributes to its reduction, without creating adverse effects in other senses, is likely to be highly valuable. Assume, very conservatively, that occupational mismatch (too many manual workers) accounts for 10 per cent of unemployment. When unemployment averages 2 million across a year, and assuming the average benefit cost to be £100/week, then the annual cost of occupational mismatch = 2m x 0.1 x £100 x 52 or about £ 1 billion per annum. Every one per cent impact on occupational mismatch would therefore be worth £10 million to the exchequer.

Discussion has hitherto mainly focused upon the potential for publicly funded adult training to help people to move across barriers from sections of the workforce having excess labour to other areas where there are shortfalls or where supply is in balance with demand. If it can be shown that adult training is capable of bringing about such moves, and that individuals and employers would not of their own accord provide such training, then the cost-benefit case for public provision appears watertight (once again, see Jackman and colleagues for demonstration). Caution would need to be exercised, however, in assessing the chances that training would, in practice, be feasible and effective. The conditions under which training provision is likely to be cost-effective is a large subject and one which lies outside our remit. But guidance could be proposed as an essential adjunct to any such policy.

The argument is as follows. If people are able to move from one occupation (or industry) to another without difficulty, then they will do so under pressure of unemployment. In that case, costly training provision is unnecessary and wasteful. It follows, then, that training is justifiable precisely where movement across boundaries is difficult, and hence where training itself is likely to be risky (that is, where there is likely to be an appreciable failure rate), where accordingly employers will be unwilling to offer conversion training, and where people are less likely to put themselves forward. Guidance then has the functions of

(i) helping to lower risks for individuals, by helping with risk appraisal and by increasing self-knowledge and knowledge of training opportunities, and thus increasing the recruitment rate to training,
(ii) helping to lower risks for public providers, and hence reduce the unit cost of provision, by helping people to make better decisions about entry to training.

The potential of guidance to fulfil these functions is, of course, something that can only be judged by experience and research.

Would there be a potential for guidance to help reduce mismatch, on its own? For adults, the potential would appear to be small but not negligible. There is already a high level of horizontal mobility (within occupational groups); upward mobility, or movement into skill shortage areas, would generally require skills training. Nevertheless, there could be opportunities through horizontal mobility and without substantial re-training, which some individuals did not take advantage of through one or other of the deficiencies in information or insight which we have previously described. Even marginal improvements would be valuable, if they could be provided at low cost. This seems to point towards possibilities for enhanced guidance facilities built into various parts of existing services.

Where guidance, on its own, could be expected to contribute to a reduction in mismatch is with young entrants to the labour market and with school-age children developing their vocational choices. There appears to be an excessive supply to lower-skilled and manual occupations among school-leavers, which pre-dates YTS/YT and may to a considerable extent have shaped and constrained YTS/YT provision. A minor, but significant, proportion of 16-year-old entrants to the labour market has achieved qualification levels at school sufficient to continue in full-time courses and to obtain entrance to intermediate occupations following vocational training. Guiding these to stay in education would be highly cost effective from the viewpoint of a mismatch analysis.

From a strictly economistic viewpoint, it can of course be argued that guidance is beside the point: people would go to the low unemployment sectors provided that the relationship between entry costs (education, training) and returns (wages) was right. However, wage rigidity is a fundamental problem of the UK economy (and of the other larger European economies as well – see OECD, 1989), so looking in that direction does not offer an easy alternative. In any case, it seems reasonable to suppose that, for many people, judgements about the entry costs to occupations, and of the returns to be had from entering them, are distorted by lack of information, by an unduly narrow consideration of the possibilities, or by difficulties in weighing up any risks involved. Guidance is intended to help individuals with all these kinds of problems; to the extent that it succeeds, it can incidentally create a margin for improvement in the wider labour market. It only needs to be a small margin to make a substantial economic contribution.

c) *Discouraged Workers*

Discouraged workers are usually defined as those who are no longer looking for work, but who would be interested in a job if they thought that they had a chance of getting one. Under ILO definitions, these are not counted as unemployed. However, surveys of unemployed claimants, and especially of stock samples covering those with long periods of unemployment, show that significant proportions of claimants have effectively ceased to look for work. There is a strong association between this condition and (a) age, with older workers particularly likely to become discouraged early in unemployment, (b) length of time in unemployment (see, for example, White, 1983).

The Labour Force Surveys, using ILO definitions, showed about 200,000 discouraged workers in the mid-80s, falling to 100,000 in the employment boom of 1988-89 (see Department of Employment, 1989a). However, discouraged workers who continue to claim are probably as numerous (see Department of Employment, 1989b), so that the total would be of the order of 200,000-400,000. On other definitions (for example, taking account of married women who would like to return to jobs, but are deterred by local rates of unemployment), higher figures could be claimed.

Evidently, discouraged workers are extremely costly. If they are claimants, then there are direct exchequer costs of benefits or income support. If they are non-claimants, there is still the loss of output to the economy, and the reduced competition in the labour market, to be taken into account. Furthermore, once a person ceases to apply for jobs, the probability of re-employment naturally drops close to zero. Research suggests that about one quarter of people with two or more years of unemployment may be discouraged workers, and that the figure for 18-24 year olds with six months or more of unemployment may be about 10-15 per cent (White, 1983; White and McRae, 1989). While difficult to quantify in any precise sense, it would be reasonable to assume that the annual exchequer cost of discouraged workers was of the order of £1 billion, and the wider economic costs at least as much again.

Discouraged workers can be pictured in terms of job search theory. They have lowered their reservation wage to the point where it is not worth looking for jobs. This in turn may be because they have developed a low valuation of their own capacities, as a result of frequent failure in job-seeking. The jobs which they think they could get would be paid at such low wages, as to be not worth looking for, once information costs are taken into consideration.

A worthwhile aim in relation to this group is to encourage them to seek jobs again. Even if they have only a low chance of actually getting a job, this will be much higher than if they make no applications at all. Furthermore, the longer the period of discouragement continues, the more it is likely to become self-confirming. The social argument is that unless help is provided, these individuals – many in the prime of their lives – may find their long-term prospects greatly damaged. A strong public policy argument for maintaining a high level of participation in job search, moreover, is that this tends to maintain downward pressure on wages, which is important for aggregate adjustment of the labour market.

What effect could guidance be expected to have on the problem of discouragement? The problem is a difficult one. People who are discouraged tend to have real disadvantages, and to a degree their evaluation of their own poor chances is a rational one. On the other hand, skilled guidance could find possibilities where individuals feel that they have exhausted them. Moreover, when a problem has become so extreme and so costly, small improvements are likely to be highly worthwhile.

Since job-search costs are likely to be crucial for this group, the first priority should be to provide opportunities which minimise these costs for the discouraged individual. On this basis, an effective form of help to discouraged workers would be to provide them with specific, selected job vacancy opportunities to apply for. Guidance specialists may see this more as the role of placement services, but there may be a need for placement and guidance to be more closely integrated in meeting the needs of clients such as these.

Some discouraged workers may be unnecessarily restricting the sections of the job market which they scan. For example, quite a large proportion of discouraged individuals are skilled workers (White, 1983), and they may limit their search to the jobs most obviously using their skills. However, it is possible that employers in other fields would be interested in employing them. A service which could steer people in the direction of such opportunities would be both enlarging job search when it had become too restricted, and reducing search costs. Rebuilding interest in job search by helping individuals to review their own capabilities (the counselling end of guidance) might also be effective, if it resulted in a redirection of efforts into possibilities which had previously been overlooked.

However, any of these steps may be easier said than done. Discouraged workers, according to our analysis, are discouraged for good reasons, and overcoming their problems may as a result require more resources than guidance on its own could be expected to supply. This example suggests, therefore, the need to consider guidance within the wider context of labour market institutions.

C. Guidance and New Institutions in the Labour Market

In Part B, the device used has been to consider how guidance could mitigate costs in relation to some specific aspects of unemployment. The particular advantage of doing that lies in the fairly specific (and large) costs which can be attached to unemployment. If we can see guidance contributing to a reduction in those costs, we can reasonably judge that its economic value is likely to be substantial.

However, these examples give a one-sided view of the potential of guidance. Guidance is also intended to support the normal functioning of the labour market and to help people at all stages. In Part B we mentioned how guidance could support the introduction of training vouchers for young people. Now we extend this approach. The aim is to examine what part guidance can play within or in relation to new institutions which are thought to be valuable. Our comments are brief, and are meant only to suggest the possibilities.

a) Training and Enterprise Councils
TECs have, among their major roles, those of delivering the major national training programmes, YT and ET, and of helping employers to get the skills they need to be competitive and efficient. These roles place TECs in an important position concerning the use and development of guidance services. Through YT, TECs are involved with the Careers Service, and as discussed earlier, the introduction of training vouchers would create a strong presumption in favour of the further need for guidance services. Similarly, a major feature of ET has been the provision of a personal assessment to clients, leading to the formulation of an individual action plan.

In developing skills provision for local labour markets, TECs may also need methods of stimulating the availability and flexibility of local skills, at lowest cost. While training will form an essential part of the provision, it may often be more cost-effective to make use of existing skills which are being underutilised. Guidance services, which serve to identify unused individual potential, and match it with up-to-date skill demands, could provide an attractive adjunct or alternative to training. Many employers might benefit from systematic attempts to identify internal skill resources. As part of such a review, individuals might be helped to evaluate their own potential and to learn about opportunities both inside their organizations and in wider careers. In short, an effective labour market needs individuals who are active seekers of training and job opportunities, and this is most likely when the associated information costs (in the wide sense of information) are reasonably low. Guidance services would be seeking to fulfil that condition.

TECs will also be intermediaries between the local labour market and employers on one hand, and the schools and other educational providers on the other. TECs are likely to play an increasing role in TVEI, Compacts, and other programmes of change, and in all of these guidance is likely to be significant (see, for example, the comments on Compacts, below).

In short, because of their central role in local labour markets and in human capital formation, TECs are also capable of having a constructive relationship with guidance services. How they develop this relationship, will of course depend upon many other factors. At the same time, guidance services might (if appropriately and cost-effectively developed) help the TECs to achieve their objectives and to balance the needs of individuals and employers.

A sensible question to ask is: what might be the penalties if TECs did not take account of guidance issues and provided no facilitation for guidance services? It would seem likely that, in that case, the main guidance services will remain in a relatively peripheral role, with respect to the labour market, as at present. In particular, there will be little chance (without the active participation of TECs in the issue) of guidance developing a strong role within adult training and employment markets. This will not appear to be a problem, if one believes that the existing markets work well, with high levels of information about opportunities, costs and returns, and flexible wages sending out appropriate signals to the economic actors to tell them when changes are needed. However, if one believes that existing information is highly imperfect, and wage signals lacking because of rigidity, then it seems clear that better guidance systems, including the provision of local market signals, should form an area of concern for TECs.

b) National Vocational Qualifications

One of the new features of the growing system of NVQs is the possibility of accrediting a wide range of work-based skills when these can be demonstrated to approved standards. NVQs offer the hope of certificated qualifications for individuals with low educational attainments, who have nevertheless acquired practical skills. They also potentially provide new motivation for workers to acquire skills, knowing that they can then be certificated. These aspects of NVQs create the possibility of new kinds of leverage on a labour market which has a high proportion of educationally under-qualified workers.

The issue of guidance, in relation to these possibilities, seems so far to have attracted little public attention. But the arguments in favour of a role for guidance would seem to be similar to those concerning training vouchers. People who are not accustomed to thinking in terms of qualifications and certification may need help in re-orienting themselves towards these opportunities and, more plainly, getting to know what they could do.

c) Compacts

Compacts, and the related Education-Business Partnerships, should have a particular relevance and interest from the viewpoint of guidance. Among the aims of Compacts is to increase motivation for young people, especially for those who find themselves in circumstances where motivation is likely to be weak. One path to achieving this is to increase contacts with the world of employment and to show what employers want from young workers. These aims and methods suggest that, in an indirect way, Compacts are very much in the business of guidance: they are helping young people to form clearer impressions of work opportunities and requirements. Particular activities within some Compacts, such as work shadowing or work tasting, can have a strong guidance component.

Some Compacts appear to be going further and directly fostering guidance activities. Should this be an explicit part of Compacts in general? It would, at the least, seem useful to follow up a development of interest in work opportunities and in educational pathways to work, by offering a guidance service which helps young people to go further with their thinking. Otherwise the economic effectiveness of Compacts could be limited in one of several ways. On one hand, a young person could fail to consolidate a general interest into a specific work-related choice. So motivation may increase, but then not be channeled in the directions originally intended, for lack of guidance. On the other hand, the work-related experiences provided through Compacts may on occasion provide an unbalanced kind of influence, leading to premature occupational choices. Systematic guidance could provide the right balance.

There seem to be some interesting questions to pursue concerning the relationships between Compacts, traditional guidance services, and innovations in guidance.

d) Open Learning

An area in which the UK appears to have a developed a lead over many other European countries is open learning (OL). In principle this appears to be a highly flexible and cost-effective method for the delivery of many kinds of education and training. Among the examples of OL in practice are the Open University, the Open College, the Open College of the Arts, the various developments sponsored under the Open Tech programme, and the uses of OL in company training provision such as at National Westminster Bank, the Rover Learning Business, etc. (for examples of the increasing importance of OL in company training programmes, see Horton, 1990).

The diffusion of OL poses interesting questions about guidance. While there has been much professional discussion of the ways in which guidance may be integrated with teaching practice, this has tended to focus upon conventional situations with classes or one-to-one teaching. How is guidance to be delivered when the student is largely engaged in self-instruction, and when learning is controlled by structured materials rather than by a teacher? One possible answer may be that, as the tutor is freed from traditional modes of instruction, he/she can acquire more scope for a guidance role. Another answer may be that there should be stronger guidance at the gateway to OL, so that users would have a better idea of the occupational possibilities or personal objectives which various OL-based courses would support. More radically, OL packages may offer self-assessment modules, computer-assisted career information systems, and so on; in short, guidance could, up to a point, be incorporated in OL.

What are the potential costs of OL unsupported by adequate guidance? To some extent they would be similar to those indicated under the heading of Compacts: a failure to convert educational motivation into occupational investment. Additionally, there could be direct costs which would detract from the cost-effectiveness potentially offered by OL. While OL rightly encourages a degree of exploratory behaviour, there may be particular dangers (through low entry costs, etc.) that it could be used in a rather aimless and unproductive way. Such a risk should be reduced through appropriate guidance support.

e) Final Comments on Guidance and Labour Market Institutions

The preceding examples could be added to in many different ways. For example, this section has largely dwelt upon young people's educational and training, but guidance may be equally important for adults considering education, training and job market choices. Indeed, it is likely that in any aspect of labour market institutions, or in any labour market initiative, guidance has or could have a role. This is consistent with our first and most general characterization of the labour market, in terms of several basic types of decisions made by individuals. Since the motive power of the labour market consists in people's decisions, it is natural that guidance (defined as a process of supporting decisions) should be applicable more or less everywhere.

It should not be supposed that people are, at present, taking their labour market decisions without guidance. Rather, a great many people within the labour market institutions presumably exercise a partial guidance role among their other activities. As a result, presumably much of the guidance received by individuals is — as noted in Section One — relatively informal or unsystematic. The issue is probably not one of whether to give guidance at all (versus no guidance whatever), but more whether there would be gains from providing more extensive professional or specialised guidance of high quality, and if so, whether these gains would repay the costs of improved provision. This type of question cannot be answered in the abstract or in general terms. It all depends on the application and the implementation. Our discussion shows the wide relevance of guidance to labour market processes, but demonstrating the value of guidance would require evaluation or monitoring studies in a variety of specific circumstances. The next section considers the available evidence from studies which have already been conducted.

Section Three: The Evidence
John Killeen

As we have just seen, there are good *a priori* reasons to suppose that guidance may have beneficial economic effects. To what extent is this confirmed by the evidence? We shall answer this question in the following steps. First, we shall contrast the volume of recent research into economic effects to the much greater volume of research into non-economic effects and attempt to show why the latter predominates. Second, we will compare the economic criteria adopted by researchers, to those implied by the economic analysis in Section Two, indicating the degree of fit and what appear to be the most important gaps. Third, we will give a brief indication of the typical research strategies, drawing attention to their strengths and weaknesses, and thus showing why greater weight is to be attached to some results than to others. Finally, we shall review the findings of this research, using the economic analysis in Section Two as a framework. Some readers may, therefore, prefer to go directly to p.59. The focus is upon British research, but where selected US materials can fill gaps, or are exemplary, we shall include them, albeit cautiously. The reasons for our caution are twofold. Most obviously (and as in all international borrowings) the danger exists that the effects of guidance may depend upon national context. The difference between the US and UK education systems is a clear case in point. Less obviously, the same or similar names, such as the US 'career education' and the UK 'careers education' conceal wide variations in practice (see p.72).

A. Trends in Evaluation
The evolution of guidance is marked by an increasing respect for the rights and powers of those exposed to it. The scientific approach advocated in the 1920s and 1930s was an attempt to put the 'matching' aspect of guidance on to an objective, expert footing. The whole procedure was conducted much as one might deploy conscripts to an army, except that instead of seeking the ideal person for the job, the aim became one of determining the ideal job for the person. The individual was an object of expert psychometric

scrutiny. Recommendations were somewhat oracular. Many of the benefits of guidance were thought to be dependent upon, or channelled through, compliance with these recommendations.

In recent decades, however, the notion of 'ideal' placement has receded: people and jobs are somewhat more elastic than the notion implies, and flexibility is, in any event, increasingly required. Greater attention has also been paid to the 'agency' of the individual to whom guidance is offered and to the individual's 'ownership' of decisions concerning his or her future. People often have fairly decided views which they bring to guidance and poorly-informed intentions are likely to be contradicted by the recommendations made to them. But what if the response is to reject recommendations, rather than adopt them as substitute goals? Expert guidance recommendations do not necessarily have an impact upon individuals' intentions. Thus it is now viewed as somewhat ritualistic to claim that benefits *would* follow *if* expert recommendations were adhered to. The more important question is 'does guidance have a real impact on the way people form and pursue their own intentions?' Guidance continues to incorporate elements of the 'matching' (or 'person-environment fit') paradigm, and advisers continue to make recommendations, but the emphasis is now upon *learning outcomes*: the development of knowledge and skills in individuals, which they can use in making their own decisions and in putting their intentions into effect, and which can be put to repeated use in the labour market. The extension of educational guidance and careers education have had a reinforcing effect. The educative approach to guidance promotes learning outcomes, designed to make individuals more effective actors in the labour market and more effective in their use of VET systems. Thus learning outcomes have come to occupy the position previously held by compliance with recommendations, as the channel through which many other benefits are thought to flow.

Figure 3.1 gives an outline of these learning outcomes. In brief, they comprise four core areas: 'self awareness', 'opportunity awareness', 'decision-making skills' and 'transition skills' (Law and Watts, 1977). They also include two further categories of frequently-evaluated outcomes closely associated with these areas: 'precursors' (relevant attitudinal and emotional changes); and 'certainty of decision' – the subjective sense of having sufficiently decided objectives to be able to act confidently upon them. A sequence of research reviews (e.g. Fretz, 1981; Pickering and Vacc, 1984) have shown that the effectiveness of guidance in relation to these outcomes is beyond reasonable doubt. The work of Spokane and Oliver (1983;

Figure 3.1:
Learning outcomes and closely associated outcomes of guidance

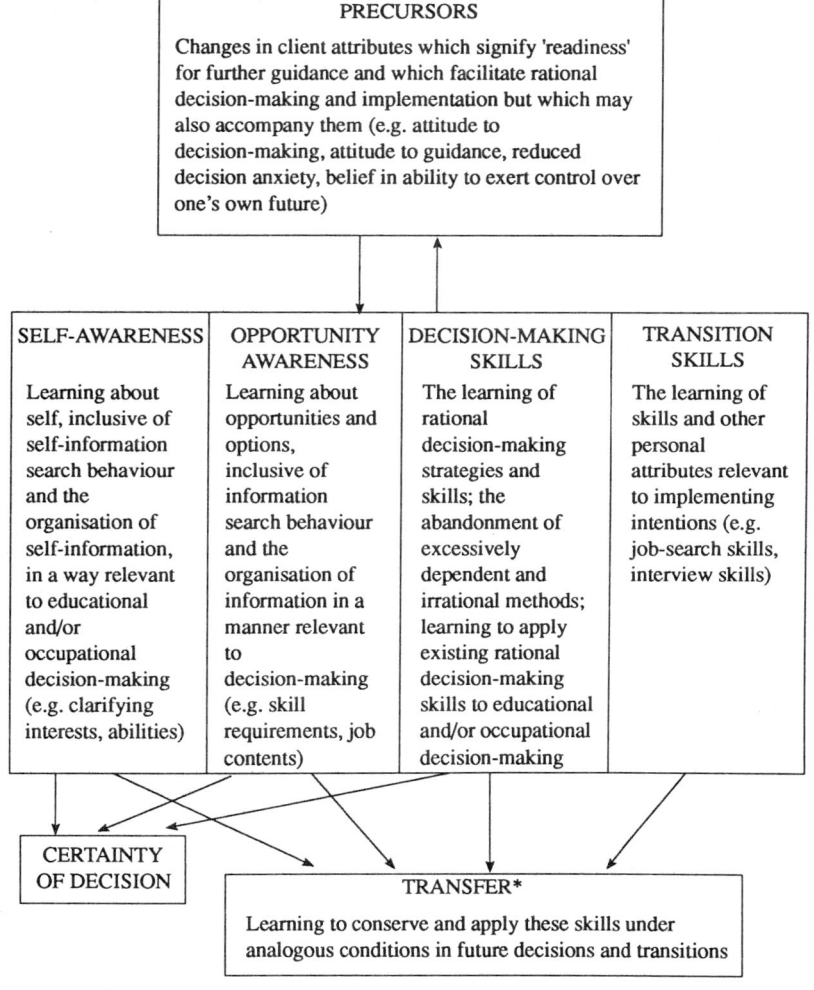

PRECURSORS

Changes in client attributes which signify 'readiness' for further guidance and which facilitate rational decision-making and implementation but which may also accompany them (e.g. attitude to decision-making, attitude to guidance, reduced decision anxiety, belief in ability to exert control over one's own future)

SELF-AWARENESS	OPPORTUNITY AWARENESS	DECISION-MAKING SKILLS	TRANSITION SKILLS
Learning about self, inclusive of self-information search behaviour and the organisation of self-information, in a way relevant to educational and/or occupational decision-making (e.g. clarifying interests, abilities)	Learning about opportunities and options, inclusive of information search behaviour and the organisation of information in a manner relevant to decision-making (e.g. skill requirements, job contents)	The learning of rational decision-making strategies and skills; the abandonment of excessively dependent and irrational methods; learning to apply existing rational decision-making skills to educational and/or occupational decision-making	The learning of skills and other personal attributes relevant to implementing intentions (e.g. job-search skills, interview skills)

CERTAINTY OF DECISION

TRANSFER*

Learning to conserve and apply these skills under analogous conditions in future decisions and transitions

* The final outcome category conforms with current conceptions of good practice and with the general philosophy of learning outcomes. Evaluation studies of learning transfer have not yet been reported.

Source: Killeen and Kidd, 1991
Classification derived from Law and Watts, 1977

revised as Oliver and Spokane, 1988) is worth particular mention in this respect. They conducted an extensive search of the US literature, accepting for inclusion in their review only methodologically adequate controlled trial studies for which full information was available on all measured outcomes. The overwhelming majority of these were 'learning outcomes'. They conducted a 'meta-analysis': a fresh set of calculations to which the results of each study contributed. They found that guidance led to an average improvement of between 15 and 29 percentile points[1]. They went on to show that (lengthier) classroom interventions had the biggest overall effect, but that individual guidance produced the greatest effect per hour. Workshops and structured groups were judged cost-effective against a simple cost measure based on counsellor-contact hours; 'counsellor-free' methods such as computerised interventions (which did produce learning outcomes) could not be included in this comparison.

These and similar findings are described fully by Killeen and Kidd (1991), who have also analysed more recent research, including that conducted in the United Kingdom. Killeen and Kidd concluded that positive results are documented for all major guidance strategies across most learning outcome types, and that the effects of successive guidance interventions on learning outcomes can be cumulative. The range of activities giving rise to these outcomes and falling within the scope of the present review include those of the Careers Service and similar dedicated agencies, the guidance work of schools and colleges, careers education, work experience (in its careers educational aspect), and various interventions for adults, such as individual guidance and 'course'-based interventions for unemployed adults and adult returners.

In comparison to the evaluation of learning effects, the evaluation of economic effects occupies a position of severe disadvantage. It is relatively easy to mount controlled trials when immediately-intended outcomes are open to observation in the short term. From the learning-outcomes perspective, guidance can be evaluated much as one might evaluate the effectiveness of an educational programme, by testing those exposed to it. However, just as it is difficult to isolate the effects on people's lives of exposure to a brief fragment of their education, so also is it difficult to assess the economic effects of particular, brief guidance interventions. Timescales are often lengthy and many mediating factors come into play. It is often unreasonable to anticipate large effects. In order to demonstrate them confidently, large samples, low rates of sample attrition over time, and rigorous methodology are all necessary. Moreover, the controlled trial technique, which permits us to distinguish effects from mere consequences, becomes increasingly impracticable with the passage of time. 'Control' cannot be indefinitely extended, nor guidance indefinitely denied.

Consequently, Oliver and Spokane (1988), who adopted rather severe rules of selection, and were, in any event, concerned only with fairly recent US research, identified only *two* studies taking economic or career outcomes as criteria. An earlier reviewer (Fretz, 1981) identified career outcomes as a category which should in principle, but seldom was in practice, considered. But to the extent that guidance is, like education, instrumental, and to the extent that the value of learning outcomes is itself judged by their economic consequences, an obligation remains upon us periodically to examine the direct evidence for economic effects. It is to this task that we now turn.

B. Economic Criteria of Evaluation

We shall begin by deriving a number of evaluative criteria from the analysis of potential in Section Two. The evaluators of guidance have always worked at the individual level, rather than the system level. This does not mean that they have been indifferent to benefits to employers, to educational institutions or to society as a whole. It merely means that they have practised 'methodological individualism'. They have, for example, looked at the wage rates of those exposed to guidance, but they have not attempted to show what effect guidance institutions may have on aggregate wage rates. Thus in considering the potential economic benefits discussed in Section Two, we must confine ourselves to hypotheses which can be tested by looking at what happens to individuals as a result of their exposure to guidance. It is important to bear in mind in formulating such hypotheses that they refer to modest but worthwhile effects which may occur if rational economic actors have access to improved information and information-processing facilities. Guidance may be associated with:

(i) Raised probability of labour-market participation, in relation to:
    (a) 'new groups' part-time and full-time (pp.13–15)
    (b) as a special case, previously discouraged workers (ppp.31–33)

(ii) Reduced under- and over-investment in human capital. This is a complex general hypothesis. More limited hypotheses are that guidance may tend to be associated with:
    (a) raised net probability of participation in post-compulsory education and/or entry into training (pp.22–27)
        (i) especially at 16+ (p.25)

(ii) especially for the purpose of cross-occupational mobility by unemployed persons (p.30)
  (b) reduced student wastage, increased pass rates and grades (p.16)
(iii) Greater congruence between abilities, etc., and jobs entered. This is also a complex general hypothesis, giving rise to the further ones that guidance will be associated with:
  (a) raised occupational skill level (p.21)
  (b) raised productivity (p.24)
(iv) More efficient job search, and thus:
  (a) reduced job-search cost (duration), with job quality held constant (p.19)
  (b) increased job quality, with job-search cost (duration) held constant (p.19)
(v) Reduced rates of entry into oversupplied occupations (pp.27–31), and hence:
  (a) raised lifetime income (relative to controls)
  (b) lowered lifetime unemployment

Figure 3.2 is a comprehensive list of the potential outcomes examined in studies inspected for the purpose of this review. It is plain from this list that even without benefit of the wider analysis provided in Section Two, evaluators have often attempted to select or devise similar indicators. Figure 3.2 also makes it plain that evaluators have had some very specific, additional indicators and ideas in mind. These are (a) job retention and turnover and (b) the degree of 'congruence' or agreement between guidance recommendations and jobs entered. We shall begin by describing these preoccupations, but continue the list to describe other categories of common criteria. We shall then look at the 'fit' between the analysis in Section Two and the most commonly adopted indicators.

The main 'economic' criteria studied have been:

(i) *Job retention and turnover*: One of the most frequent assumptions has been that mobility rates and patterns provide reasonably accessible, objective indicators of (or act as a proxy for) a range of other variables which it would be difficult or impossible to measure objectively in a mass follow-up of those exposed to guidance. This has usually been the case in studies of new entrants to the labour market. It has been assumed that if the job entered immediately after exposure to guidance is acceptable to the individual, and if the

Figure 3.2: Economic criteria and mediators adopted as outcome variables in studies of the effects of guidance

1. JOB RETENTION AND MOVEMENT/TURNOVER (FREQUENCY)** (O)
   Increased job retention, lowered frequency of movement, taken to signify appropriate 'matching'. Hence AS A PROXY FOR
   - employee acceptability to employer (productivity, etc.)
   - job acceptability to the employee (satisfaction, etc.)
   - reduced employer turnover costs (search, training, etc.)
   - reduced job search costs (inc. income foregone)

   Hence frequency of movement taken as an index of 'floundering' in the labour market.

2. JOB MOVEMENT/TURNOVER (QUALITY)
   Increase in *proportion* of all movements which are classified beneficial/neutral as follows:
   - UPWARDS (O)
   - WITHIN OCCUPATION (O)
   - TO CONGRUENCE WITH RECOMMENDATIONS* (O)
   - TO CONGRUENCE WITH MEASURED INTERESTS (O)

   Each taken as an index of progression etc., thus being the converse of 'floundering'. Also
   - FOR REASON OF REDUNDANCY, ETC.* (O)

   taken to signify 'involuntary' separation on part of employer and employee, and hence unassociated with poor job performance, dissatisfaction, etc., in comparison to dismissals, voluntary leaving. (But 'mismatch' ignored. See pp.27–31.) Also
   - SATISFACTION WITH PROGRESS (S)

3. CONGRUENCE RATE
   - WITH RECOMMENDATIONS* (O)
   - WITH MEASURED INTERESTS (O)

   as an index of 'matching', hence see description of proxy assumptions at (1) above. (Measured ability, etc., used to generate experimental group recommendations, but congruence with measured ability has not acted as a criterion.)

4. INCOME* (O)
   - WAGE LEVEL* (O)
   - INCOME SATISFACTION (S)

5. OTHER SATISFACTION MEASURES
   - WORK ITSELF (INTRINSIC) (S)
   - GLOBAL JOB SATISFACTION** (S)
   - SUBJECTIVE SENSE OF SUCCESS (S)
   - SELF-ESTIMATED SUITABILITY* (S)

   often taken as proxy for productivity, etc.

6. DISCIPLINARY
   - DAYS LATE (O)
   - ABSENTEEISM (O)
   - INCIDENCE OF DISCIPLINARY PROCEEDINGS (O)
   assumed to be proxy for productivity/performance
   (See also reasons for job separation at 2. above)

7. EMPLOYER-RATED SUITABILITY* (S)
   (taken as proxy for productivity, etc.)

8. EDUCATIONAL PERFORMANCE
   - BASIC SKILLS ACQUISITION (English, maths, etc.) (O)
   - DROP-OUT PRIOR TO COMPLETION OF COURSES (O)
   - PASS RATES* (O)
   - GRADES* (O)

9. WAIT/SEARCH, UNEMPLOYMENT AND INVOLUNTARY NON- OR SUB-EMPLOYMENT
   - REDUCED UNEMPLOYMENT RATE** (O)
   - REDUCED UNEMPLOYMENT DURATION** (O)
   - AS ABOVE, BUT INCLUSIVE OF NON-EMPLOYED (etc.) JOB SEEKERS

10. AS (9) AND
    - RAISED OPEN EMPLOYMENT RATE** (O)
    - RAISED RATE OF ENTRY TO VET (US CETA Programs only)
    - RAISED RATE OF ENTRY TO TRAINING-RELATED INDUSTRY (US CETA Programs only)
    - RAISED RATE OF ENTRY TO 'GROWTH' AREA (US CETA Programs only)
    - TO MORE 'SKILLED JOB' (US CETA Programs only)
    - JOB QUALITY (INCOME; SOCIOECONOMIC STATUS; JOB SATISFACTION) RELATIVE TO PAST JOB/CONTROLS.

11. AS (9) AND HENCE
    - WELFARE PAYMENT SAVINGS
    - WELFARE PAYMENT SAVINGS MINUS COST OF GUIDANCE PROVISION

Notes
1. Many of the above variables are infrequently adopted as criteria, and several appear only in one or two studies. Regularly employed criteria are marked with a double asterisk (**). Criteria employed on several occasions are marked (*).
2. Objective measures are marked 'O', Subjective measures 'S'.
3. A general supposition exists that most of these outcomes imply mutual benefits to individuals and their employers or educational institutions. A further general supposition of public benefit is also often made.

individual is productive and acceptable to the employer, then this will be reflected in lower job separation rates and increased tenure. It follows that the incidence of job-search costs and employee-replacement costs are also reduced. Evaluators have had in mind studies which associated 'turbulence' or 'floundering' with higher frequencies and overall durations of unemployment, entry into jobs without training, and other disbenefits. But even to the earliest researchers, this appeared to be something of an over-simplification, since complete immobility was plainly an unrealistic and undesirable goal. They reasoned that when job separation does occur, the *reasons* for this should be more consistent with good initial matching in samples of individuals exposed to guidance. Early on, attempts were made to consider this issue, although it must be conceded that the difficulties of the task were not fully appreciated and that data were incomplete and of suspect validity.

Attempts have also been made to define reasonably objective, standardised measures which encapsulate the idea that some job moves are consistent with a good initial match. Upward progression and job movement within, rather than away from, the kind of work initially entered have both been employed in this way. Other sorts of job moves have been treated as beneficial, such as movement towards work more consistent with measured interests. Even in the very earliest studies, a similar measure was available. Given that job recommendations were based upon measured abilities (together with other data) movement towards greater 'congruence' with those recommendations was treated as movement into work to which the individual was better fitted. This is a potentially circular contention, of course, and we shall consider 'congruence' in a little more detail below. But to summarise, it has often been assumed that guidance should diminish, but not expunge, job mobility and lead to 'better' forms of movement.

(ii) *Congruence*. Agreement (variously called congruence, accordance and concordance) between recommendations and the first job entered after guidance has also been a major criterion of evaluation. Early evaluators assumed that the degree of congruence between recommendations and jobs entered said something about the adequacy of guidance procedures. If one form of guidance was associated with more 'congruence' than another, then perhaps its diagnostic procedures were more accurate and its recommendations both more enthusiastically received and more realistic. We shall examine the limitations of this view later (p.56). However, 'congruence' has been incorporated into more complex criteria. This has been on the principle that the benefits of guidance should be proportional to the degree to which recommendations are followed. Thus job retention, salary level and other measures have been examined *in conjunction with* congruence. But as we shall also see, where controlled trials cannot be conducted, 'congruence' has continued to offer an alternative basis for comparison, to that between experimental and control groups.

(iii) *Reward measures.* That evaluators should seek directly to measure the rewards of guidance goes almost without saying. From an economic viewpoint, income is a crucial consideration, and wage level (an objective criterion) has been employed. However, subjective satisfaction measures have been more common. Such measures are often viewed as a summary statement of the benefits and disbenefits arising from work, and thus of the full range of utilities which economists are prepared to acknowledge in principle, but do not generally seek to measure.

(iv) *Productivity measures (employment).* Evaluators seldom use the word 'productivity'. When they do so it is not clear that they mean the same thing by it as would an economist. They have measured wage rates, for example, but they have not treated these as signifying productivity. Ironically, the closest approach to an economist's conception is made when doubts are expressed over the use of initial wage rates as a measure of the effectiveness of guidance. This is on the basis that trainee rates may be lower than unskilled ones. More often, evaluators have in mind the idea that individuals perform better or worse in the jobs that they actually enter. They have approached this issue in a variety of ways. Job retention and the reasons for job change may be thought to be associated with performance. Sometimes it has been thought that job satisfaction acts as an oblique measure. Meta-analyses of the relationship between job satisfaction and job performance indicate that the relationship is significant, but weak ($r=0.23$ (Petty *et al.*, 1984); $r=0.17$ (Iaffaldano and Muchinsky, 1985)). Self-ratings and employers' ratings of 'suitability' have also been used. The difficulties facing evaluators here are considerable. Follow-up studies to individuals entering numerous occupations in many places of employment are forced to rely upon highly simplified subjective judgments of performance. It is difficult to know how valid these are. One of the very earliest evaluators (Earle, 1931) became convinced in the course of his study that small employers (who predominated) adopted a highly protective stance when asked such a question about their young employees.

(v) *Productivity measures (education)*. In comparison, fairly clear and unambiguous measures of educational performance exist, and these have been readily available. Evaluators have been able to capitalise on the assessment routinely undertaken in educational institutions. But this has usually been in the United States, and the form of intervention examined against such criteria has usually been much broader than careers guidance as we have defined it.

(vi) *Unemployment and its alternatives*. The avowed aim of many guidance initiatives has been to offer assistance to the unemployed and others seeking work. Thus re-employment rates, unemployment duration and associated measures have been self-evident criteria in numerous evaluation studies. A handful of studies, to which we shall draw attention, go on to consider the *quality* of subsequent employment thus recognising the potential trade-off between job search duration and wage level. Only one study has considered public cost savings.

Figure 3.3 summarises what has been said so far. There *are* areas of agreement between the most obvious requirements of the economic analysis given in Section Two, and the existing body of research. This is so especially in relation to the efficiency of job search, employment chances and reward levels. Evaluators have also attempted to assess productivity in employment (usually construed as performance) by indirect and/or subjective means. Any weaknesses in the latter regard are due to the inherent difficulties of the task, rather than to reluctance to confront the issue. But Figure 3.3 also makes it plain that substantial gaps exist in our current knowledge. This is not a black-and-white matter. In some areas (ability utilisation; productivity at work) our knowledge could be greatly improved, but perhaps the most important omissions are:

(i) The capacity of guidance to induce non-participant groups to enter the labour market (e.g. women returners, discouraged workers).
(ii) The influence of guidance on education (and training) participation rates.
(iii) The ability of guidance, as offered prior to human capital decisions, to influence student wastage and achievement.

Figure 3.3: Correspondence between preferred outcome indicators and the available evidence

PREFERRED INDICATORS	AVAILABLE EVIDENCE
Probability of labour-market participation • New groups • Discouraged workers	No direct evidence. Some unemployed samples likely to include discouraged workers, but these not separately identified.
Probability of participation in VET • Post-compulsory education • Job with training • Retraining	No direct evidence Some US studies of guidance for the unemployed include entry into education/training as one of a range of positive outcomes.
Productivity (education and training) • Level of qualification • Educational wastage (non-completion) • Pass rate • Grades	Most evidence refers to student counselling interventions inclusive of, but not confined to, careers guidance, which are concurrent with, rather than prior to, the course of education in question. Most of this is of US origin.
Occupational skill level	Sometimes indirectly indicated by socio-economic status and job-quality rankings. Some relevant data available in early studies of scientific guidance.
Productivity (in employment)	Job retention and reason for job movement widely used as a proxy. Also job satisfaction. Employer ratings of 'suitability' etc. Occasional use of disciplinary indices, but only in US studies of broad guidance interventions, inclusive of but not confined to careers guidance, offered to current employees. Wage rates sometimes available but not consciously used for this purpose.
Efficiency of job search • Duration • Job quality	Job-search duration a common outcome variable in studies of guidance interventions for unemployed adults (also non-employed). Simultaneous consideration of job quality sometimes occurs (income; job satisfaction; socio-economic status). Job retention used as proxy for subjectively perceived job quality. Some information on income and self-rated job satisfaction in early studies of young people. Qualitative features of job mobility also used as an

	indicator of impact on efficiency of job search. (Indirect evidence arises from relative rate of use of formal guidance agencies as routes to employment by social groups excluded from informal information networks.)
Probability of entry to undersupplied job sectors • Lifetime income • Lifetime unemployment	No direct UK evidence. Income and employment chances considered only in the shorter term permitted to follow-up studies. Some data sets exist which would permit calculation of the propensity of careers officers to disapprove intentions to enter oversupplied sectors, but such analyses have not been made.

(iv) The role of guidance in leading individuals away from areas of labour surplus.
(v) Effects on lifetime income.
(vi) Effects on lifetime unemployment.

It would be wrong to view these gaps in our knowledge as an indictment of past evaluators. Often they have studied groups, such as minimum-age entrants to the labour market, for which particular provisions have been made. This has in turn made it impossible to ask some of the foregoing questions (for example, one cannot assess the effect of guidance on full-time educational participation, if one studies provision specifically directed to labour-market entrants). In addition, the timescale required to address some of these questions is very great. And of course, only an analysis of the kind undertaken for the first time in Section Two allows us to see with any clarity where the gaps may lie. Evaluators have been responsive to the policy preoccupations and programme objectives of which they have actually been aware. Subject to these limitations, even the very earliest studies provide at least some evidence which remains relevant to us today. But how has this evidence been obtained? It is to this question that we now turn.

C. Strategies in the Evaluation of Economic Benefits

We are concerned here with what is called *summative* evaluation: that type of evaluation which attempts to draw conclusions about the effects of guidance. In practice, it is difficult to draw a clear dividing line between this and *formative* evaluation, which provides commentary and feedback to those who are engaged in development, and which often includes opinion data.

For example, approximately 20,000 pupil-years of secondary education are now annually devoted to work experience. Beneficial effects are repeatedly attributed to it by participants, teachers, and the employers who provide places. But our requirement is, plainly, for more firmly-based 'conclusions', and we must set such opinion data aside. What are the typical strategies for collecting summative evidence, and how effective are they?

(i) *Case studies.* Selected longitudinal case studies have often been employed in the attempt to demonstrate or illustrate the effects of guidance. Super's (1957) highly influential text contained several, including one of a client who was helped to cope with a conflict between her attempt to conform to scientific role expectations and an emergent pattern of interests focusing upon service and interpersonal activities. She was advised to take an educational route which was consistent with her tested abilities but which kept both options open. She was also advised to engage in exploratory activities which would allow her to develop a clearer self-concept. As a result, she eventually entered work of a non-scientific (social) character. Super judged the intervention successful against three of the criteria discussed earlier: supervisor-rated job performance was good, the client was satisfied in her job, and she was soon promoted.

But are case studies of this kind an adequate test? Each is, in effect, an uncontrolled longitudinal study of a sample of one. Since it would be futile to report randomly selected case histories, the accumulated evidence of many such studies may be regarded as reflecting a highly biased sample. Moreover, the guidance may not have 'worked' in the way claimed, and even if the guidance intervention really did 'work', a suspicion remains that *similar* outcomes *could* have arisen in its absence. The method is not ultimately, therefore, a convincing one.

(ii) *Representative longitudinal studies.* Designs of this kind answer the first of these criticisms of the case study, but not the second. All or a defensibly representative sample of those exposed to a guidance intervention are studied, and the frequency of defined outcomes becomes an obvious consideration. The implication of this approach is often that *change* is being sought, and studies may be divided into those which do, and do not, effectively demonstrate this change. Four types of design can be distinguished within this category.

(a) *Implicit pre/post-test designs.* It is often unnecessary to take special steps to measure the initial (pre-test) condition, because it is in all

relevant respects uniform. This is most obviously the case of guidance intended to result in the re-employment of the unemployed.
(b) *Explicit pre/post-test designs.* When guidance is intended to influence variables which do not adopt a uniform, known value at the outset, measurement of their values prior to guidance is an obvious requirement[2]. One of the few examples of such a study in its more-or-less pure form (i.e. without a control group) is Bedford's (1982) examination of the rate of learning gain during vocational guidance interviews with careers officers[3]. When we turn to economic outcomes, 'before and after' measurement is most commonly included in studies of the effect of student counselling on academic performance, or as part of the assessment of re-employment interventions. In the latter case, this is in order to determine whether enhanced employment chances are brought about by the reduction of job quality. However, there are two characteristic failings associated with designs of this general type. These are described as (c) and (d) below, each by means of an example.
(c) *Follow-up against inadequately defined initial conditions.* Wankowski (1979) followed-up the floundering and poorly-performing undergraduate clients referred to an educational counselling service: taking their eventual graduation rate as his criterion. In this study, the initial condition was not precisely defined in such a way that it could be measured in the same way at a later date. By implication, educational performance improved, but one cannot quantify this improvement.
(d) *Retrospective measurement of initial conditions.* Pearson (1988) evaluated a bridge programme for unemployed managers and professionals. He gathered his data on earlier salaries and job satisfaction by asking those who subsequently became employed to make better/worse comparisons. The imprecision of this procedure should be self-evident. More to the point, here, however, is the question-mark which hangs over the retrospective reporting of highly subjective states such as job satisfaction.

Designs (a) and (b) cope well, and (c) and (d) rather less well, with the problem of demonstrating *gains* on outcome measures in populations or representative samples of those exposed to guidance. They do not, however, address the question of the *effect size* of guidance, or of the value it adds. It is one thing to observe a change, another to show that guidance has produced it, and yet another to show that it would not have been produced by other means, if guidance had been withheld[4]. The classic method for doing so is the controlled trial.

(iii) *Controlled designs and alternative treatment trials.* Three designs can be distinguished here:
(a) *Random assignment.* It is widely understood that the controlled trial is a method for examining the effects of an intervention (or 'treatment') by contrasting what happens to those exposed to it (the experimental group) to a 'control' group. It thus makes good the chief deficiency of simple longitudinal designs. (The statistical controlled trial is, however, made up of a family of designs[5], united by the use of random assignment to 'experimental' and 'control' conditions, and all that this entails[6].) The most obvious criterion for judging the technical adequacy of any evaluation which calls itself a 'controlled trial' is that random assignment has actually occurred.

Studies of guidance which fulfil this criterion differ in two chief respects. First, they do or do not 'match' pairs of individuals, prior to random assignment, thus ensuring to an even greater degree that experimental and control groups are similar. Second, they may demonstrate effects 'post-test only' (which is to say, only on the basis of a comparison between groups *after* the intervention) or on a 'pre/post-test' basis (by comparing measurements made before and after the intervention, between groups). The latter design usually increases the precision with which effects can be judged.

Uncomplicated examples of the 'post-test only' design tend to be confined to studies of learning outcomes. For example, gains in career maturity (Crites, 1974) have been shown in this way for work experience (Pumfrey and Schofield, 1982) and a life-role planning course (Amatea *et al.*, 1984).

Turning to 'pre/post-test' studies we find that, as in the case of follow-up studies, the design can be implicit or explicit. It is implicit when the initial value of the outcome measure is uniform and known, as in earlier examples of interventions for the unemployed. The rapid spread of the 'Job Club' approach to the guidance of adults in the United States[7] is, at least in part, attributable to the careful way in which its originators designed their evaluative studies and, especially, to their determination that genuinely random matched-pair assignment to 'experimental' and 'control' groups would occur (e.g. Azrin *et al.* 1975). So why aren't *all* controlled trials like this? We shall now see why this is so.

(b) *Weakened control designs.* Studies of guidance, like other studies of 'real life' activities, such as education, often face the problem that random assignment is not possible or permitted. Existing groups, such as careers education class groups, may be the irreducible units with which one must deal. Those exposed to guidance may be self-selecting. It is particularly the case of studies of economic effects that, for these sorts of reason, true statistical experiments seldom occur. The best that can usually be hoped for is that broadly comparable groups, or deliberately selected 'matching' individuals, can be used as weak controls.

Such studies exist in plenty. Hopson (1970) compared the early labour market experiences of an age cohort leaving a school after the introduction of careers education, to the leaver cohort of the preceding year, which acted as a control group. Fairbairns and Coolbear's (1982) study of the effectiveness of an individual guidance programme for unemployed adults was based upon *post hoc* matching of control subjects to volunteer experimental subjects. Pearson's (1988) study, which has already been described, involved a comparison of the re-employment rate of those exposed to a course-based guidance intervention to the general rate: a weak form of control.

(c) *Alternative treatment trials.* One of the main problems for evaluators has been the ubiquity of access to formal guidance, particularly for young people. This has meant that 'no-treatment' control has often been difficult. When this has been recognised, alternative formal guidance treatments have deliberately been compared. Sometimes new or unconventional practices are added to or substituted for the conventional procedures to which 'controls' are exposed. In other respects, such studies may be statistical or 'weakened' comparisons of the kinds described above. Some of the earliest studies of guidance were, in part (see later), alternative treatment trials. Earle (1931) and Hunt (née Allen) and Smith (1932; 1944) took as their controls young people exposed to the existing provisions for school leavers.

Alternative treatment trials do not directly estimate the effectiveness of guidance. However, trivially few studies of any kind demonstrate negative effects (Spokane and Oliver, 1983). Thus the discrepancy between the effectiveness of the most and least effective guidance in any trial can, with reasonable confidence, be treated as a likely underestimate of the effectiveness of the former. This is rather like saying that in a 'no treatment controlled' trial, formal guidance provision has to add its effects to those brought about in control groups by the 'informal' sources (family, friends, etc.) to which most of us are exposed.

(iv) *Congruence designs.* A method of particular importance in the evaluation of guidance from the 1920s to the present day has been the 'congruence design'. It represents an attempt to kill two birds with one stone. In the absence of control groups, the congruence design provides an alternative basis for comparison. Furthermore, it follows the logic of an 'expert matching' approach to guidance, thus providing (in the eyes of those who offer such guidance) a fair test of effectiveness.

Those exposed to 'expert matching' guidance are subsequently separated into two groups: clients who follow guidance recommendations (the 'congruent' or 'concordant' or 'accordant') and clients who do not (the incongruent). Economic and associated outcomes are then compared across groups. If guidance works, then levels of benefit should be greater in the 'congruent' group. Congruence designs are thus tests of a mechanism whereby guidance is designed to have its effects.

There are, however, some indications that the manner in which individuals are classified as congruent influences results. One of the first evaluators (Earle, 1931) tried to resolve this problem by using a five-point scale of congruence, but most of his comparisons were actually based on a very stringent definition. In comparison, other early evaluators used more generous definitions (e.g. Burt *et al.*, 1926; Allen and Smith, 1932; Hunt and Smith, 1944). Thus it is unsurprising that they found more congruence. Less expectedly, however, they tended to find higher 'returns' to congruence. In Burt's study, it is plain that this is because those judged congruent on a strict or a loose definition fared equally well. Later studies of congruence with Careers Service advice (Cherry, 1974; Thomas, n.d.) are susceptible to a similar observation, in the sense that common procedures were not adopted.

But this aside, what are the more general limitations of the congruence approach? In the absence of a control group, we are not free to infer that gains have actually been made in the sample as a whole. Congruence may fortuitously predict the distribution of benefits. This could happen if the sort of people who comply with recommendations are also the sort of people who tend to report themselves satisfied with their jobs, or who tend to be immobile, etc. It could also happen if cases of congruence clustered in 'good jobs'. But setting aside such possibilities, and assuming that guidance recommendations represent correct diagnoses of the occupational types to which each individual is best-fitted, a doubt continues to exist. Perhaps individuals do not follow recommendations, so that congruence is a matter of coincidence? In this event, guidance would predict the future without exercising an influence upon it[8].

The Evidence

(v) *Multivariate and compound designs*. As we have just seen of simple congruence studies, it is possible to generate alternative explanations of apparent guidance effects. This applies to all follow-up studies, and the conventional riposte is the controlled trial. However, as we have also seen, it is often necessary to mount such trials in a 'weakened' form. Even in statistical trials, it is not possible to exert control over access to guidance in the long run. For these and other reasons[9], a 'multivariate' element enters into some studies. This is the direct measurement and incorporation into analysis of factors which may obscure or artificially inflate results.

From the earliest times, some studies of the effects of 'congruence' were *also* random-assignment alternative treatment trials *and* 'multivariate', in the sense that they attended to the 'good jobs' hypothesis (Earle, 1931; Allen and Smith, 1932). The advent of computers and the application of more powerful statistical techniques has led to the more elegant treatment of the 'good jobs' hypothesis and to extension of the range of competing hypotheses to include the two other possibilities we have just described ('sorts of people' and failure to heed recommendations, see p.63) (Cherry, 1974).

Indeed, given that control is often weak and sometimes non-existent, it is difficult to overstate the importance of the application of multivariate techniques. This point can be driven home by giving two brief examples of studies in which this did not happen. Both were evaluations of JIIG-CAL, a computerised careers guidance system widely used in British schools. In one study (NFER, 1987) comparison groups were formed by taking large samples of children in relatively modest numbers of schools in which JIIG-CAL had and had not been adopted. This form of weakened control inevitably gives rise to a question about the other differences between the schools involved. No attempt was made to measure such differences and incorporate them in the analysis. In a second study, Closs *et al*. (1985) undertook a comparison between experimental and control groups, partitioning the former into those most and least influenced by JIIG-CAL. The most influenced were defined as those who seriously considered a JIIG-CAL recommendation, went on to enter it and remained in it at the three-year follow-up stage. Comparisons therefore included a 'congruence' element, but in comparison to Cherry's study, this one was highly retrograde. Not only was no correction explicitly made for prior intentions, but what has hitherto been taken as an outcome (job retention) came to be incorporated into the definition of JIIG-CAL's 'influence'. This exaggerated the possibility that the 'good jobs' hypothesis might explain any apparent differences between groups.

There is no reason in principle why an exclusively 'multivariate' approach to the evaluation of guidance should not be attempted. This means the abandonment of experimentation, and turning instead to the diversity of existing provision as the basis of comparison. The amount and kinds of guidance to which similar individuals are actually exposed varies. Thus data-sets which capture this variation, together with other relevant differences (mediating factors; 'competing hypotheses') and relevant economic outcomes could in principle be analysed in order to expose the effects of guidance. The chief reasons why this has seldom been attempted seem to be: first, the 'habit' of experimentation; second, the need to await recent developments in techniques of analysis; and third, the poverty of existing data sets, when compared to what is required. To date, therefore, only two or three studies of this kind have been attempted, none of which is entirely satisfactory. In the United States, Hill (1989) used administratively available data in an unsuccessful attempt to isolate the contribution of guidance to the success of rehabilitation programmes for the visually disabled[10]. Also in the United States, a similarly unsuccessful attempt to assess the contribution of guidance was made in a small, *ex post facto* (retrospective) study of 'Comprehensive Employment and Training Program' participants (Rodenstein, 1982)[11]. In view of the various deficiencies of these early attempts, when set against what is required, their results are not particularly discouraging. We shall argue in Section Four that a more refined multivariate approach has an important role to play in the future of guidance evaluation.

Conclusion. Whilst we envisage a future role for the 'multivariate' approach, preference is given in our review of past research to controlled trials. This is, however, with the caveat that in the longer run control groups are likely to have access to guidance. This leads us to suppose that the effects of guidance are more easy to demonstrate in the short term, and to anticipate 'wash-out' – the tendency for experimental and control groups to converge with the passage of time. Non-controlled follow-up data based on representative samples are a useful adjunct, particularly when observed patterns are similar to those demonstrated by unrepresentative experimental groups. But where control has been weak or nonexistent, preference is given to evidence which has been subjected to cross-examination by the multivariate (or competing hypotheses) technique. Comparisons based on congruence are, similarly, more convincing when subject to cross-examination or when made in the context of controlled trials. It is with these priorities in mind that we now turn to the evidence.

D. The Effects of Guidance

In order to make a reasonably orderly exposition of the evidence, it is necessary to avoid going into too much detail. (Notes at the end of our report point to technical difficulties which bear upon interpretation, amplify some of our reasoning, and give a number of results in precise terms. General conclusions are given at the end of each of the longer subsections which follow.) We shall begin by assessing the proposition that congruence has acted as a mechanism to distribute benefits. We shall then examine the evidence for supposing that guidance promotes economic benefits. For as we have seen, congruence studies alone cannot answer this question.

(i) *Congruence*. Congruence studies examine only one of the 'mechanisms' of guidance. But any guidance which makes recommendations, or which examines individuals' intentions with a view to their approval or disapproval, can he considered in this way. We shall focus on congruence studies which have looked at scientific guidance and careers officers' suggestions. The only congruence study to have examined options generated by a computer program (JIIG-CAL) seems to us best set aside for reasons already given (p.57).

The earliest congruence studies were conducted amongst minimum-age school leavers and on samples of somewhat older entrants to the labour market who were voluntary clients of the National Institute for Industrial Psychology (NIIP). They looked at psychometrically-based 'scientific guidance'. Burt *et al.*'s (1926) study of 100 minimum-age leavers was to set the tone for those that followed. Two years after guidance the young people were found to be divided approximately equally into two groups, one in recommended occupations or occupations judged similar to recommendation, the other not. Members of the former group were more than twice as likely to be satisfied with 'work, pay and prospects', and twenty times less likely to be dissatisfied with the 'work itself'. Thus at the subjective level, the job rewards of congruence seemed considerable. At the objective level, however, matters were less clear-cut. The average wages of the congruent group were 7% higher than those of the incongruent one (this may not be statistically significant, and data were not reported which allow the appropriate calculation). Turning to another objective measure (the role of which as an assumed proxy for other benefits has already been described – see p.44–47), initial job retention was greater in the congruent group: 57%, as opposed to 39% entering non-congruent occupations, remained in their initial posts. Similarly, 'rapid job changing' was much less: only 2%, as opposed to 12.5%, changed employers three or more times.

Burt *et al.*'s study was, therefore, encouraging, especially with regard to subjective measures of reward and the impact of congruence upon job retention. But data were gathered from parents rather than directly from the young people themselves, thus calling into question the subjective reward measures which gave rise to the most striking findings.

Subsequent studies considered larger samples, and in any event, increased the total number of individuals examined. Burt *et al.*'s success in obtaining follow-up data (92% at two years) was, however, to remain unequalled. Improvements were made in the measurement of congruence and, crucially, information was collected directly from those who had been exposed to guidance. A succession of follow-up studies of NIIP clients (Macrae, 1932; 1933; Jennings and Stott, 1936; Handyside and Stott, 1958)[12] continued to show that in the early years of employment, subjective expressions of satisfaction (job satisfaction, or liking for work; sense of making progress, or 'doing well') were twice as frequent for those in occupations congruent with the recommendations made to them. As already suggested in our discussion of a rather different sort of study (see p.58), this effect apparently 'washes out' in the longer term. A follow-up 30 years after guidance was unable to demonstrate such an effect, although this was in a modest sample subject to heavy attrition (Farid-Uddin, 1971).

Thus NIIP client follow-up studies supported the conclusion that congruence is associated with higher subjective reward levels in the early years of employment. But only one of these studies (Lancashire, 1971) considered job movement patterns. In a ten-year follow-up to 116 young men advised to enter engineering above technician level, Lancashire found that those who had done so enjoyed a higher ratio of upward to other job moves – that is, that they experienced less 'floundering change' (see p.47). This study is not in itself a sufficient guide, of course, since horizontal movement may be more characteristic of other occupational areas than it is of engineering. Our conclusions concerning job movement must, therefore, be based upon the studies of minimum-age leavers which followed on from that of Burt *et al.*, and to which we now turn.

Three alternative treatment-trials provided evidence about congruence (Earle, 1931; Allen and Smith, 1932; Hunt – née Allen – and Smith, 1944). Each compared the effect of congruence with scientific guidance recommendations, to that of congruence with the conventional form of advice, offered to a quite different (randomly assigned) 'control' sample, by the

Juvenile Employment Officers of the day. Earle's study was conducted in London, those of Hunt (Allen) and Smith in Birmingham. As noted earlier (p.56) Earle defined congruence more stringently than Hunt (Allen) and Smith. Thus Earle reported 'less' congruence and weaker congruence effects[13]. The relative rates of congruence between experimental and control groups, and changes in these rates over time, also differed[14].

For these and other reasons[15], it is unsurprising that the London and Birmingham studies disagreed in other respects. In Earle's study, job satisfaction was associated with congruence in both samples. Like Earle, Allen and Smith (1932) found it associated with congruence in both samples, though more strongly so amongst the scientifically advised. Later (1944) they found a much more striking disparity. 'Congruent' individuals were three times more likely to say that their jobs were suitable, but this was *only* true of the scientific guidance sample. Amongst controls, a weak reverse trend was observed. Employers' ratings of suitability (which have been thought a measure of performance – see p.48) were positively associated with congruence only for the scientific guidance group, but high levels of non-response mean that this result should be treated with circumspection.

Earle found congruence to be associated with job retention in both samples. However, those entering directly into 'most congruent' jobs, whilst fewer in number in the sample exposed to scientific guidance, remained in them to the end of the study more often[16]. Neither of the Birmingham studies was able to show this effect in control groups. Amongst the scientifically advised, though, it was dramatic. In the 1932 study, congruent first jobs were eleven times more likely to be retained over a 2.5–3 year period. In the later study, in which samples were much larger, but subject to higher rates of attrition, congruent first jobs were five times more likely to be retained for two years, and four times more likely to be retained for four years.

To summarise, early studies of school leavers confirmed the results of those of NIIP clients. Congruence was associated with (increasingly adequate) measures of satisfaction or perceived job suitability; in one study, this extended to employers' ratings. This research also indicated an effect on job tenure during the first years of employment. Congruence appeared to have a particularly substantial effect on tenure of the first posts young people entered. In two studies out of three, marked advantages to those entering occupations congruent with scientific guidance recommendations failed to find an echo amongst those entering jobs congruent with the recommendations of conventional advisers. But in Earle's study, modest benefits arose for both of these groups. Sufficient methodological differences exist to make it uncertain whether these disparities are 'artefacts', or represent real variation in the conventional provision available at the time, or are attributable to some other factor, such as local labour-market dissimilarities. What do more recent studies of 'conventional provision' tell us?

It may be quite artificial to treat the 'recommendations' recorded by careers officers and their predecessors (the only other practitioners for whom evidence of this kind is available) in the same way as scientific guidance recommendations. This is not a matter of the extra time and resources sometimes put into alternative experimental interventions. An element of artificiality would enter into evaluation if the *status* of 'recommendations' were to be wrongly construed. Perhaps young people and their parents have already formed their intentions? Perhaps 'recommendations' record intentions? Earle (1931) acknowledged that this was often so in conventional guidance practice. More recently, and so far as the educative approach is adopted, perhaps the careers officer is more concerned to help those who have adopted unrealistic or unduly modest objectives to explore further? Perhaps, where no objectives are present, the careers officer seeks to address the client at his or her own 'starting point', rather than rush to a recommendation?

But congruence studies can be justified in two ways. The first is on the rather weak grounds that controlled trials of an ubiquitous statutory provision are difficult to mount and that therefore an alternative must be found (see p.55). The second is on the rather stronger grounds that the Careers Service seeks to identify young people in need of extra or special attention. Thus if one distinguishes between young people who do and do not already have intentions, and between guidance recommendations which do and do not 'approve' these intentions, the basis exists for a more elaborate form of congruence study, which tests careers officers' diagnostic ability. Sillitoe and Meltzer (1985) provide evidence concerning the predictive validity of careers officers' recommendations. They offer data for 269 matched pairs of Afro-Caribbean and white school leavers, all holding vocational intentions at the time of CO interview. Among all whites, 75% of intentions were approved, and approved intentions were two and a half times more likely to be realised than disapproved ones. For 'early migrants', predictions were somewhat more accurate because COs were less 'lenient' as to level of aspiration when set against ability[17].

But the main evidence available to us comes from studies by Cherry (1971; 1974) and Thomas (n.d.). Both Cherry and Thomas distinguished between 'following 'recommendations' and the pursuit of pre-existing intentions. This is a major advance on pre-war studies. As we have already seen (p.57), Cherry also addressed two further difficulties. The first is the possibility that congruence or concordance effects are, in fact, the effects of entry into what are popularly regarded as 'good jobs'. She did this by comparing across occupational levels, finding congruence effects at each level (but see below). Second, she attempted, by means of the Maudsley Personality Inventory, to examine the possibility that those who enter concordant and discordant jobs are 'different sorts of people'. Again she found no significant difference, but this was, of course, a far from exhaustive examination of group differences.

Cherry's study was of a sizeable sub-sample[18] of 1961 school leavers from the 1946 National Survey of Health and Development cohort and made a complex series of comparisons[19]. To summarise, Cherry was able to find a congruence effect, and was able to show that this was not simply because 'recommendations' recorded young people's intentions. Discordance between COs' recommendations or 'approvals' and the first job entered doubled the rate of early job leaving[20]. Where COs disagreed with existing intentions, either as to field, or occupational level, early job-leaving rates were raised. Allen and Smith (1932) had earlier found that 52% of 'non-congruent' scientifically-advised boys had entered unskilled jobs and that their job-separation rates were high. Cherry found that boys entering jobs below the skill level recommended by COs had very high early leaving rates.

The results of Thomas' (n.d.) study of a large sample of boys depart from those of Sillitoe and Meltzer (1985) and Cherry (1971; 1974). As in our comparison of early studies, a sufficient number of technical differences exist[21] to make the precise reason for disagreement unclear. Briefly, Thomas found a much weaker connection than did Sillitoe and Meltzer between COs' 'approval' of young people's intentions (i.e. non-suggestion of alternatives) and subsequent entry into the job-type in question. Perhaps associated with this, he found that the 'approval' of COs did nothing to enhance the effect of entry into an intended occupation upon job retention (to eighteen months). Indeed, 'approval' was associated with a somewhat higher rate of subsequent rapid job changing (3+ jobs) in this group. His findings were thus also at variance with those of Cherry (1971; 1974), described above. Thomas concluded that adherence to an early intention and entry into that occupation was the key factor determining early job retention.

He did, however, show that those who had no fixed intention, or who failed to enter an occupation they intended, fared better if they adopted a CO recommendation, rather than entering some other type of occupation.

Thus *on balance*, the evidence suggests that 'approvals' made by careers officers enhance the predictability of entry to intended occupations. Their approval, or following their suggestions, is associated with increased job tenure. This seems (on balance) either to resolve disagreements between prewar studies about such effects or, alternatively, to point to improvements in the predictive validity of recommendations, since the days of Juvenile Employment Bureaux. The evidence simply does not exist, however, which would allow us to resolve early disagreements about congruence effects on job satisfaction and similar outcomes. But it seems quite clear that congruence with 'scientific guidance' has been associated with both job retention and job satisfaction (or similar measures) during the early years of employment. The chief criticism to be made of this genre of investigation is, however, the generally crude way in which it relates to current guidance processes and the arbitrary (and sometimes fortuitous) elements which enter into the design of its tests. But even supposing the evidence of congruence studies conclusive, we still do not know if guidance is effective. It is to effects that we now turn.

(ii) *The role of guidance in improving the efficiency of job search and reducing unemployment.* Several kinds of evidence are available to us, which we shall consider in sequence. First, an important category of indirect evidence suggests that formal guidance channels communicate information more widely than would otherwise be the case, thus raising the employment chances of special groups. Second, an 'alternative treatments' trial in a graduate Careers Advisory Service indicated that the manner in which guidance is offered can influence job search duration. Finally, we shall look at the major body of evidence which arises from studies of guidance for unemployed and non-employed job-seekers, and (upon occasion) guidance for those at risk of unemployment.

First, then, we will examine *formal guidance channels and widened access to information.* For many years it has been supposed that a high proportion of job information flows along 'informal' channels. This leads, in turn, to the supposition that socially excluded groups, whose members are not part of the networks along which this information flows, may be at a competitive disadvantage in relation to the ability and skills they have to offer to employers. One of the arguments in favour of formal, public guidance channels is that they may redress the balance, providing wider access to information. Members of recently immigrant ethnic minorities are repeatedly characterised as excluded from informal channels, and numerous studies of their transition to work have shown two equally important things. First, as the earlier argument would indicate, these groups are indeed more reliant upon formal guidance agencies as channels to their first employment. Second, this is not because they confine their job-search activity to these formal agencies; it is simply because other channels are less productive for them than for the majority population (e.g. Sillitoe and Meltzer, 1985; Dex, 1978; Lee and Wrench, 1983).

Thus a *prima facie* case exists to suppose that by providing wider access to information, formal channels reduce unemployment durations amongst those excluded from informal networks. There is, however, a complication which must be considered. The claim is sometimes made that formal channels communicate information about different, less desirable opportunities, to that communicated by informal ones. This is associated with the belief that formal channels tend to be used by those with weaker labour-market characteristics[22]. In effect, therefore, some socially excluded groups (and especially ethnic minorities) may simply be finding their way to the forms of employment open to them in a discriminatory labour market, which in practice means using the channels employed by less-able whites and accepting reduced job quality in comparison to whites of similar ability.

So does greater reliance on formal channels reduce job quality? Ideally one would like to compare the relative job quality of members of ethnic minorities to that of matching members of the majority population and these, in turn, to the channels through which jobs are obtained. This calculation has not (to the author's knowledge) been made, and we are thrown back on weaker and indirect evidence. Sillitoe and Meltzer (1985) used the subjective criterion of entry to 'desired occupation'. They showed that amongst the 'high' academic attainment group, the Careers Service functioned equally well for Afro-Caribbeans and whites, whereas 'other' channels delivered 'desired occupations' more frequently to whites. However, this pattern did not hold for those of moderate and low academic achievement. In these categories, both the Careers Service and 'other' channels delivered a higher proportion of 'desired occupations' to whites than to Afro-Caribbeans. This disparity between ability levels is suggestive of aspirational differences. Overall, the results are inconclusive, but the reduction of racial disparities amongst the most able by a formal guidance agency argues at least a modest widening of access to information, rather than an exclusively channelling effect[23].

Moreover, the underlying assumption, that formal guidance agencies are specialised channels which transmit information to individuals with inherently weak labour-market characteristics, does not seem tenable. We can use duration of education as an indicator of these characteristics. The 1981 NCDS sweep (Ives, 1985) showed formal channels to act as the route to first employment for an equal proportion (one-quarter) of minimum-age leavers and of those leaving education at a later age. A similar proportion of university graduates use formal channels (Williamson, 1981), and the more prestigious the higher educational establishment, the more likely is it that placement will occur through its advisory service (Boys and Kirkland, 1988). It could be argued that despite this overall pattern, formal agencies are of greater importance to those with weaker labour market characteristics within each general category. But Raffe (1985) has shown by analysis of Scottish School Leavers data that leavers of a wide range of academic abilities are placed by the Careers Service to 'all but the most senior' white-collar occupations. So it is not inevitable that able, but socially excluded people, who use formal channels to find jobs, must purchase increased employment chances at the cost of entry to jobs normally held by those with inherently weak labour-market characteristics. Hence, formal channels may also lead to more efficient utilisation of the available stock of ability.

We now turn to more direct evidence in terms of *graduate job-search duration*. Most of the experimental evidence relating to the enhancement of job search and reduction of unemployment is derived from studies of interventions for adults. One study bridges the gap, being concerned with those about to graduate. The study is an exceptional one of its kind, since most experimental and quasi-experimental studies of guidance for students are American, take educational performance as their general criterion, and refer to a form of intervention (student counselling) which includes a careers guidance element, as we have defined it, but is also concerned with personal issues and learning difficulties. Goldman's (1976) alternative treatment study took in all arts graduates of a British university over a period of three years. Goldman's criterion was 'early decision' or cessation of job search[24], and her intervention was unequivocally 'careers guidance'. Those about to graduate who had unclear/multiple vocational goals (about two-thirds), but who received only one guidance interview, had a low probability (28%) of being 'early deciders'. However, those with clear goals having only one interview, and those without clear goals having two or more interviews, did equally well (81% v. 82%). The inference is that a strategy which actively encourages vocationally uncertain persons to return for further interviews (and to engage in appropriate tasks and pursue appropriate intermediate goals) raises *overall* 'early decision' rates.

Goldman tested this contention by gathering data over a three-year period. In the first, two careers advisers adopted conventional procedures. In the second, one adopted the recommended strategy, whereas the other merely made a general offer of further interviews to all clients without encouraging the undecided to take advantage of the offer. In the third year, both advisers adopted the recommended strategy. Early placement rates in the first and third years were similar, but lower in the second year, and in that year the relationship between interview frequency and early decision-making was broken for the adviser not adopting the recommended strategy. Thus Goldman's study appears to indicate that the conventional practice of year one was similar in its effects to the specific form of her recommended intervention. In effect, the study appears to indicate a return to good practice.

Further direct evidence relates to *adult job-search duration*. There is clear evidence of widespread demand for guidance in the general adult population (Alloway, 1986; Killeen, 1986). This demand is not confined to unemployed and non-employed job-seekers (Arbeiter *et al.*, 1978; Killeen, 1986). However, most of the available evidence about effects relates to these categories, although there are some US studies of employer-led initiatives for those in employment. Some of the latter (outplacement counselling; counselling of employees at risk of dismissal) are plainly directed to the reduction of eventual chances of unemployment, even though those exposed to them are employed. But most studies of these initiatives are descriptive, and evaluation has either consisted of unsubstantiated assertions (e.g. Papilia and Kaminsky, 1981) or been confined to the systematic reporting of opinion data (for reviews, see Cairo, 1983; Russell, 1991). Schlossburg and Leibowitz's (1980) study of a 'job separation' programme for NASA employees is an exception. This was judged successful against the criterion that, at three months, all participants were either internally re-assigned, had found new jobs, or had decided to retire. Most studies of interventions for unemployed and non-employed persons seeking work have taken a similar form, being non-controlled follow-up studies.

A review of several US and Canadian studies of *group* interventions for job search reported placement rates in the range 62% to 95% (Amundson and Borgen, 1988). But apparent success rates can conceal a great deal. For example, an 'abbreviated' job club achieved a lower rate (50%) in a very small (n=23) sample; however, reasons for cessation of search included return to education and pregnancy (Chandler, 1984). At the opposite extreme, Hesse (1982) reported the 'unsubsidised employment' of 92.6% of those completing an intensive job search course involving training, homework, social reinforcement and supervised job seeking. But only 19.9% of referrals attended and completed the course.

Trials involving a comparison are at a premium. In the UK, Pearson (1988) described a 'bridge' programme for unemployed managers and professional people. The intervention emphasised (optional) group vocational guidance and job-getting sessions, but included additional elements. Pearson gave 'known' re-employment rates (at six months) for the 'Bridge programmes as a whole' as 92%: adjusting for non-response, this exceeded the re-employment rate 'for the unemployed in general'. However, programme participants had relatively strong labour-market characteristics and included fewer long-term unemployed than the general unemployed population. Davison (1986) evaluated an individualised, short-duration (six-session) intervention for the long-term unemployed, from which the highly undecided were excluded. The intervention included target setting, confidence building measures, help with CV and letter-writing, and attempts to boost application rates. A job-entry rate of 31% was achieved, this being double the normal Employment Department caseload success rate.

Studies such as these are encouraging, but we have been at pains to point out that comparisons to population parameters are a rather weak form of control. We therefore give great emphasis to the results of controlled trials of two methods: the Job Club; and individual guidance.

In the United States the Job Club method[25] has been experimentally evaluated with a variety of client groups. Azrin *et al.* (1975) formed matched pairs of volunteer job seekers not on unemployment benefit, by means of an index of employability based on age, sex, race, education, marital status, desired occupation and salary level, number of dependents and current financial resources. Pairs were randomly assigned to intervention and control groups. The median period elapsed before entry into full-time work was reduced from 53 to 14 days, and the percentage entering full-time employment was raised at one, two and three months (at three months it was 92%, compared to 60% of controls). The rationale for excluding those on unemployment benefit in this study was a motivational one. However, a subsequent study of unemployed subjects in receipt of welfare payments compared the effectiveness of Job Clubs with that of conventional employment service counselling (Azrin *et al.*, 1980; 1981). Overall employment rates were 62% for Job Club participants, against 33% for controls. Excluding de-registrants (some of whom were already employed), these rates increased to 80% and 46% respectively. For those followed-up to 12 months, 87% of Job Club participants and 59% of controls had attained employment. Job Club cost per placement was estimated at 167 dollars (exclusive of premises). Based upon one trial site only, a comparison of welfare payments was effected (n=84 experimental and 84 control subjects). At six months, mean monthly payments had reduced by 48% (100 dollars) for Job Club participants but only 15% for controls. Although not calculated, this seemed to indicate a net saving.

Individualised trial schemes have been experimentally evaluated in the United Kingdom, although the extent to which they comprise guidance, narrowly conceived, varies. An experimental career counselling programme for PER registrants employed a weakened control design (Fairbairns and Coolbear, 1982). Experimental volunteers (n=99) were matched *post hoc* to controls. The volunteers were exposed to individual counselling and given 'homework', interview training, and limited support in the production of CVs. This led to increased numbers of job applications (compared to controls) and an exactly proportionate increase in interview offers. A small gain in new paid employment was also produced at three months (experimental subjects 57%, controls 41%) which (on incomplete follow-up data) washed-out by twelve months. An alternative way of representing these results is that a median reduction in unemployment duration of approximately two weeks was achieved.

However, even though Fairbairns and Coolbear and, to a greater degree, Azrin and his colleagues have been able to demonstrate significant gains in employment, what of job quality? In the former study, old job/new job wage and satisfaction comparisons did not differ between experimental and control groups. In Pearson's (1988) study, no evidence of 'trading down' was discovered: 63% said that their financial situation was 'better or the same' and 85% made this claim for job satisfaction (but see p.53). Azrin *et al.*'s (1975) experimental subjects demonstrated significantly higher salary and socioeconomic status than those of their matched pairs who became employed (their mean starting salary was 36% higher). Thus job search was more efficient against the complementary criteria of search duration (cost) and job quality.

To conclude: the run of results suggests that interventions inclusive of guidance intended to raise employment chances can work with a *wide range* of clients, from the long-term unemployed to the non-employed. 'Job quality' does not appear to be depressed. The results also suggest that intensive group (social reinforcement) methods may be more effective and more cost-effective than individual methods. But as we saw earlier, individual guidance has been associated with shortened job-search amongst undergraduates for whom no comparative data exist on group methods. As we also saw, indirect evidence exists that formal guidance channels raise the employment chances of those excluded from informal information networks.

(iii) *Job retention and turnover.* The role of this family of measures as a proxy for less easily-measured benefits, and the limitations of this approach, have already been discussed (see p.46). Evidence is available for three types of intervention: 'scientific guidance'; 'careers education'; and (from the United States) employers' initiatives, in the form of 'realistic job previews' and employee counselling programmes. We shall concern ourselves only with the British evidence[26].

So dominated were early British evaluators by the congruence method, that even when they mounted controlled (alternative treatment) trials, they failed to make global comparisons between experimental and control groups. The question uppermost in their minds was: 'Is congruence more beneficial in the experimental group?'. We are more concerned with the question: 'Did the experimental group benefit as a whole?'. Some new calculations can be made on the basis of early published results, and it is these that we first consider.

All three of the earliest controlled-trials show a small beneficial effect for the enhanced (scientific) guidance intervention. Earle (1931) was unable to find any overall differences in the reasons given for leaving jobs, but amongst both boys and girls, the mean number of jobs held over the trial period was lower for experimental subjects than for controls. Similar overall results were obtained by Hunt and Smith (1944) over both a two- and four-year period[27]. Average durations of posts followed a similar pattern, being nearly two months greater in the experimental group at each stage. Retention of first job throughout the trial period (Allen and Smith, 1932) and to two and four years (Hunt and Smith, 1944) was greater in the experimental groups. In the earlier study, which was subject to only modest sample attrition, the difference was narrow (33% of experimental subjects, compared to 28% of controls), occurred in a small sample, and was not statistically significant. In the later larger-sample study, the gap was wider (at four years 39% of experimental subjects, 26% of controls). This was statistically significant, but substantial sample attrition introduces an uncertainty not accommodated in the calculation of significance. It is the consistency with which a modest effect upon job retention was observed across all three studies which is the most persuasive factor, particularly when we take into account the fact that these were 'alternative treatment' trials. The effect of the experimental intervention was additional to that of the conventional forms of guidance to which young people were exposed.

It is therefore of some significance to note that more recently, when the National Child Development Survey (NCDS) cohort entered the labour market, short-term (to three months) and longer-term retention were somewhat higher amongst those placed into employment by formal guidance agencies (the Careers Service, college careers services) than amongst those entering employment through other channels (Ives, 1985). This does not directly measure the impact of guidance, much of which is provided without the immediate object of making placement possible. And of course, these are survey data, not the results of a controlled trial. They do, however, amount to one more piece of circumstantial evidence supporting the proposition that guidance exercises a modest influence upon job retention. Hopson's (1970) small-scale weakened control trial of the impact of careers education was unable to make a similar demonstration with respect to retention of first job (over a one-year period), although there was much more job-changing in his control sample. This was because control group members who changed jobs did so significantly more often. Hopson also demonstrated that 'floundering' change (defined as change of occupational area) was significantly more frequent in the control group. In addition, a higher proportion of control group subjects gave movement to better jobs as their reason for job leaving. It is unfortunate that more studies of this kind have not occurred. But we must conclude on the evidence as it stands. This indicates that not only intensive 'scientific' guidance, but also careers education and placement through guidance agencies, exerts an influence on early job retention and/or the character of early turnover patterns consistent with better initial job selection.

(iv) *Performance and participation in education and training.* Most studies which consider educational performance are American, and from the present perspective, are too confounded to be useful. By 'confounded' we mean that the intervention under evaluation often includes a careers guidance component, as we define it, but goes much wider than this, so that we are not able to isolate the specific contribution which careers guidance makes. In the US, 'career education' includes what we in the UK think of as careers education and guidance, but also a number of other features, such as basic or remedial numeracy and literacy training. The same general point applies to US 'work experience based career education'. In the US educational system generally, student counselling includes careers guidance and guidance for educational decision-making, but personal counselling and educational counselling (in study methods, etc.) often predominate (see Watts and Herr, 1976). Wide definitions have been applied in British research, with a similar effect. Nelson-Jones and Toner (1978) created a ten-item measure of (retrospectively perceived) help by the 'staff in the last educational institution you attended', and correlated it with A-level performance in a study of entrants to a single university. One may doubt the validity of such a scale, and question its application to a sample in which the range of the outcome variable is likely to be restricted. The null results of the study are thus unsurprising. But even if a positive effect had been found, we should have been little the wiser, since only three of the items on the scale referred to guidance as we have defined it.

A further difficulty is that even in their own terms, many studies are inadequate. US reviewers of 257 career education evaluation reports (most unpublished) judged only ten of them adequate against a checklist for comparative trials (Hamilton and Mitchell, 1979). British studies of careers guidance as we have defined it, which include educational outcomes among their criteria, are all methodologically flawed, inadequately reported, or both[28].

For these reasons we shall be brief. Some of the early US studies of counselling and student performance reviewed by Campbell (1965) were well-designed, and tended to show a positive association between exposure to counselling, academic grades and graduation rates. To take a later example, in a weakened control trial[29] Brown (1965) showed gains of 25% to 50% on academic performance measures. We have already briefly described a UK study (Wankowksi, 1979) which made (only) a *prima facie* case for such effects (see p.53). 56% of the poorly-performing undergraduates referred to a university counselling service did eventually graduate. But careers guidance may scarcely have entered into this or the other interventions to which we have alluded. In comparison, the counselling offered at the University of Minnesota in the late 1930s included a substantial guidance component, as we have defined it. Williamson and Bordin (1940) compared 400 counselled students to well-matched but non-random controls. Counselled students achieved significantly better grades. Campbell (1965) conducted a 25-year follow-up study (response rate 82%). He found that those exposed to counselling had a 25% higher eventual graduation rate (BA and above). Two studies of JIIG-CAL (NFER, 1987; Closs *et al*., 1985) have been criticised elsewhere (see p.57, see also note 28). Methodological caveats aside, those using JIIG-CAL whilst choosing school subjects believed themselves to have been helped by the system. In schools using JIIG-CAL fewer young people switched options (7%, compared to 10%). This can be viewed as a special form of reduced student wastage. But retrospective satisfaction with option choice was greater in control schools, which renders the results somewhat equivocal (NFER, 1987). In Closs *et al.*'s (1985) study, those in full-time education three years after exposure to the system were more satisfied with that education than were controls. If we assume a connection between satisfaction and performance, then this is indirect evidence in favour of guidance.

Turning from performance to participation, occasional studies indicate that careers educational interventions may have the incidental effect of raising educational participation in a rather specialised way, by motivating those in compulsory education to attend (e.g. Hamandi, 1977; Reed and Bazalgette, 1983).

Thus there is, from our perspective, no evidence concerning the influence of careers guidance on participation in post-compulsory education and training, but a slight indication that 'voluntary' participation during compulsory education may be enhanced. There is exceedingly weak evidence concerning the impact of guidance on option choices. Direct evidence concerning educational performance is 'confounded', and of US origin. Studies do not exist which have addressed the contribution of careers guidance head-on, in a methodologically acceptable manner.

(v) *The influence of guidance on job quality.* We shall consider two aspects of job quality, namely job satisfaction and income. Earle (1931) and Hunt and Smith (1944) continued to disagree. In Earle's study, the general distribution of job satisfaction (liking) did not differ significantly between the experimental group and controls, although slightly more of the former (5%) were 'highly' satisfied (controls, 2.9%). Thus no extra benefit accrued to scientific guidance, over the conventional form. Unlike Earle, Hunt and Smith (1944) employed standardised ratings of job 'suitability'. Assessed against all posts held, a similarly trivial difference was found[30]. But at four years, this gap had widened: 29% of current control sample jobs were unsuitable, but only 20% of those held by the experimental group. This widened gap is consistent with their other findings and is statistically significant, setting aside sample attrition.

Hopson's (1970) weakened-control study of the effects of careers education does not help to resolve the issue. Those exposed to an intensive careers education programme entered jobs congruent with their measured interests twice as often (69%) than controls (33%): a highly significant result. But Hopson was unable to demonstrate a corresponding effect upon job satisfaction. Pearson's (1988) study of an intervention for the unemployed did, on the face of things, indicate improved job satisfaction, in comparison with the jobs held prior to unemployment (85% characterised their job satisfaction as 'better or the same'). However, we have already listed certain reservations (p.53), to which we now add the observation that those about to become unemployed may not experience much satisfaction. We therefore regard the proposition that guidance leads to gains in job satisfaction as not proven, despite the relationship generally found to exist between congruence and job satisfaction[31].

Studies of young people have tended to set aside wage levels, for reasons already outlined (p.48). The evidence deriving from studies of adults is perilously slender. Pearson (1988) reported the financial situation of the new jobs obtained by those exposed to bridge programmes for the unemployed as 'better or the same' on 63% of occasions: an equivocal result. Only Azrin *et al.* (1975) offer encouraging results. Job Club participants achieved mean starting salaries 36% above those of matched controls, with corresponding gains in measured socio-economic status. This is, therefore, the only study which convincingly demonstrates a gain in job quality. But one study, no matter how well conducted, is an inadequate basis upon which to base large claims for guidance as a whole.

(vi) *Desiderata*. Three desiderata need to be considered:
(a) *Performance*. Only two (by now familiar) British studies have considered the effect of guidance upon performance, as assessed by employers' ratings of 'suitability' rather than through job retention, reasons for job movement, or job satisfaction. In brief, Earle (1931) failed to demonstrate a gain for scientific guidance over conventional procedures. Hunt and Smith (1944) found a small difference in favour of those who were scientifically advised. At two years, 28%, compared to 23% of controls, were rated 'very suitable'. At four years, this disparity disappeared, but response rates by employers at this stage were so low as to make the information almost valueless.

(b) *Industrial sectors*. We simply do not know if guidance diverts people towards areas of job growth. Only two studies offer related evidence. A persuasive campaign including a careers guidance element, aimed at reducing sex stereotyping amongst Australian girl school leavers, was associated with a raised rate of entry into trade occupations during its first year, though this diminished thereafter (Pryor, 1985). Placement to job growth areas is one of the objectives of US 'Comprehensive Employment and Training Programs'. As we have already seen, a rather crude small-sample retrospective study (Rodenstein, 1982) was unable to disentangle the contribution of guidance.

(c) *Public cost savings*. The most obvious (but not the only) public cost savings attributable to guidance result from diminished unemployment. The utility of re-employment to individuals and their families is not confined to income gains. There is, for example, no shortage of evidence about the deleterious (net) effect of unemployment on psychological well-being, as measured by psychiatric screening devices. Similarly, we might claim that the public costs of unemployment extend beyond social security payments and tax revenues foregone. In a searching examination of the costs of unemployment we might, for example, be tempted to consider what part of health expenditure is attributable to it. However, the consideration of these matters by evaluators has been negligible. Only Azrin *et al*. (1980; 1981) have attempted to estimate public cost savings. Based upon one trial site only, a comparison of welfare payments was effected between 84 Job Club participants and 84 matched controls. At six months, mean monthly welfare payments were reduced by 48% in the former group, but only 15% in the latter. This monthly mean difference (68 dollars) does not take revenue gains (taxation) into account, and must be set against Job Club costs, which Azrin *et al*. did not fully consider.

E. Conclusions

We began by assuming that the effect of formal guidance on economic outcomes would be modest. Formal provision adds to what is already there. It has always been the case that 'experimental' interventions have to make their voices heard against the background hum of 'informal' guidance. But from the earliest time, they have also had to raise their voices above those of the other formal procedures already in place. In view of this, evaluators have often failed to consider samples of sufficient size, or to pay sufficient regard to the requirements of measurement and design, or to be sufficiently inventive in circumventing the practical obstacles which stand in the way of research designs of the most routine kind. Thus a high proportion of studies which fail to demonstrate that guidance has economic effects could not reasonably be expected to do so. Equally, some studies which do demonstrate effects give rise to the nervous apprehension that, if better conducted, they might not have done so.

But here, as at earlier points in our exposition, we must attempt to form a judgment on the evidence as it stands. First, there can be little doubt that 'congruence' is associated with job retention and other criteria adopted by evaluators. Moreover, the balance of evidence favours the view that guidance practitioners' judgments predict eventual job entry and job retention. But we do not propose to dwell upon the effects of congruence, for the reasons given at the outset of our discussion. Studies of 'congruence' are only one way of investigating the mechanisms of guidance, and it is arguably of much greater importance that learning outcomes should in future come to play the 'intervening' role in research designs.

We can regard the duration of unemployment as (for all but discouraged workers) a period of job search. Thus studies which assess the role of guidance in reducing job-search duration and reducing unemployment often fall into the same general category. Studies adopting these criteria, which include some of the best-designed, strongly favour the view that guidance has beneficial effects. Job-retention and job-changing rates are often taken as proxies for a wide range of economic outcomes which it is more difficult to measure directly. These include general job quality and performance. The evidence strongly suggests that guidance increases early job retention and diminishes rapid and 'floundering' job movement. The case that guidance raises 'job satisfaction', as measured by simple self-report, is not proven, and insufficient direct evidence exists concerning wage levels. We can, however, be reasonably confident that guidance does not raise employment chances by depressing job quality: an exemplary study has shown that it can raise both employment chances and wage levels. Adequate studies of the impact of guidance as we define it on participation and performance in education and training have not been conducted, although fragmentary indications of benefit exist, which should spur us to mount studies capable of testing such effects in a more conclusive manner. Other omissions are listed on p.49–50. Future assessments of economic effects should desist from the use of subjective and overly indirect objective measures, replacing them with objective measures of the kind we have indicated. In the final section of our report we will expand upon this conclusion.

Section Four: The Future of Guidance Evaluation
John Killeen and Michael White

Our recommendations for future study of guidance follow quite directly from what we have said so far. We need to know *what* to measure. We need to choose *appropriate general strategies* in keeping with what we are measuring, and the general magnitudes of effects we anticipate. Finally, we need to be *realistic* about the way in which we will be able to implement those strategies.

We shall focus most of our attention on steps which could be taken in the short-to-medium term in order better to understand both the economic effects of guidance and the manner in which they are produced. But there is a longer-term goal which, we believe, should have an equal claim upon our attention. We suggest that over the longer term, the effectiveness of guidance will depend upon what we call a 'culture of evaluation'.

A. A Culture of Evaluation

Both the increasing importance of evaluation, and the difficulties we are likely to encounter, can be illustrated by a brief allusion to the way in which guidance is changing. Most of us are familiar with the idea of guidance for 'transitions': movement across institutional or organisational boundaries from one stage of education to another, from education to the labour market, and at later stages, between employers and employment statuses. The simplest conception of guidance is as a specialised information channel associated with 'transition' and placement, and this was indeed the form adopted by the earliest agencies. Many later developments in guidance, such as the emergence of careers education, were originally oriented to particular transitions, even though not directly concerned with placement. But as we noted in Section One, some guidance now adopts what may be called a 'system management' role. In complex employing organisations, of the sort which economists call 'internal labour markets', career development guidance may be offered with the object of promoting labour flexibility. In VET systems, too, guidance is increasingly seen as integral – as a means of allowing systems to work effectively, and for individuals to 'navigate' them, rather than as something directed overwhelmingly to transition *out* of the system in which it is provided. Developments of this kind make it less easy to think of guidance as an 'extra', and lead us to think of guidance as playing an important role in the way systems work. This reinforces the importance we attach to the evaluation of guidance. But there is an attendant difficulty, which is particularly emphasised when we consider economic effects. The more integral guidance becomes to systems, the less easy (or realistic) is it to consider its effects in isolation and in exclusively 'post-transitional' terms, and the more closely its ultimate effects become bound-up in the effectiveness of the human resource policies or VET provision in which it is embedded. We need more evaluation of guidance 'inside' systems, but we should not suppose that this will be easy to achieve.

In part, evaluation is a matter of assuring the quality of provision: of selecting and applying the right techniques with the right client groups, dependent upon local circumstances. In part, it is a matter of being accountable to sponsors: of demonstrating effectiveness, rather than counting inputs, or even counting outcomes with which the inputs may – or, more to the point, may not – be associated. But a major goal should also be to promote both innovation and the diffusion of innovation. This will require a cultural change: incentives to demonstrate effectiveness, rather than the formal adequacy of provision; tools which allow effectiveness to be demonstrated at low-cost but in a technically acceptable fashion; and access to the techniques of evaluation.

This is what we mean by a 'culture of evaluation': guidance agencies and practitioners monitoring and improving their techniques against adequate criteria, and in communication with one another. Plainly, a role exists for government, professional bodies and academic institutions in bringing this climate about: the present report is, we hope, a contribution to this process.

B. An Outline Strategy

The most basic tools which we can provide, as we have already suggested, are measures of the criteria of evaluation. But to these we need to add process measures: measures of the guidance inputs. We can encapsulate the chief problems confronting us in quite simple terms:
(i) learning outcomes are, from both a technical and a cost perspective, relatively easy (in principle) to assess, but the devices we need in order to measure learning gains are relatively difficult to formulate;

(ii) economic outcomes are, from both a technical and a cost perspective, relatively difficult to assess, but the measures we have in mind are relatively straightforward.

Thus it would be a much easier task to evaluate local programmes and procedural innovations against learning outcomes, *providing* that adequate measures existed. Whilst not wishing to rule out direct economic evaluation, we regard it as unlikely that this will routinely occur; and as we have said, we regard it as desirable that evaluation should become a routine feature of guidance practice.

We accordingly think it likely that economic assessment will be a national and less frequent activity. It thus becomes a matter of some importance to inspect the connections between learning outcomes and economic ones. If these could be established, it would underwrite the more routine use of the former. We therefore need to regard this as another priority for action at the national level.

But in each case, we think it unrealistic to indulge fantasies about a massive, long-term, dedicated study. It is, in any event, a dangerous course of action to put all of one's eggs in one basket. Thus we shall advocate addressing these sorts of concern in more general labour-market studies, and as part of the assessment of specific policy initiatives in which guidance is perceived to play an important role.

The first steps along this road are to devise appropriate measures or indicators, and (with a view to cost-minimisation) to inspect existing data-sets to see if they contain at least some data suitable for secondary analysis. We believe that 'input' and economic measures will be relatively easy to formulate, but we believe that it will be a less simple task to devise learning outcome measures suitable to our general purpose. We therefore believe that such measures should be devised in parallel with the direct economic assessment of guidance, with a view to a final round of studies which address the mechanisms through which guidance produces economic effects, and which might thus underpin low-cost, routine evaluation. We shall now outline these ideas in a little more detail.

C. What Should We Measure?
We believe that we have gone a good way towards clarifying the sort of 'economic' outcomes we should measure. Indeed, from the perspective of instrumentation, they pose fewer problems than any other category. They include participation rates in education and training, student/trainee wastage

and achievement, entry to job-growth/labour-shortage areas, job search duration, and job quality (especially objective measures). It is worth observing at this point that these are not outcomes which impose very lengthy timescales on evaluation. It is also worth noting that they need to be taken together. For example, guidance which raises wage rates in the short term may do so at the expense of participation in VET, and guidance which leads to participation in VET may do so at the expense of raised failure rates.

Certain other outcomes are, however, somewhat more problematic. It is not realistic to assume that lifetime income or lifetime unemployment can be considered directly. But this does not prevent us from considering income and unemployment in the shorter term. If we also consider occupational skill level, and take this together with the outcomes we have already listed, then we will have created a reasonable basis for projecting lifetime effects. The reasoning behind this claim has been given in Section Two.

Finally, we should consider what may be done to gauge the capacity of guidance to encourage groups such as women returners and discouraged workers to enter or re-enter the labour market. The chief problem here, of course, is that exposure to guidance may signify that entry to the labour market is already under way. However, this is really a matter of research design, rather than of instrumentation. The criteria are clear enough.

Turning to the measurement of guidance processes or inputs, this also poses relatively few difficulties, in the sense that it is fairly easy to envisage what should be measured. But the practical difficulties are much greater. We have to distinguish here between two kinds of evaluation: first, the sort of 'formative' evaluation which is associated with innovation and the improvement of techniques; and second, the sort of 'summative' evaluation which has concerned us in this report. In formative evaluation, the description of processes (or inputs) assumes considerable importance. If guidance innovations are to be replicated, and if the ways in which they achieve their effects are to be scrutinised, then adequate descriptions must enter the public domain.

But for summative purposes it is not strictly necessary to know how guidance works. What one really wants to know is: 'does guidance, as now practised, produce the effects we envisage?'. The simplest measure (and one which would permit cost-benefit analysis) would be its cost. Individuals' exposure to guidance would be measured monetarily. But this would be difficult to do directly: as we saw in Section Three, Oliver and Spokane (1988) used counsellor-hours as a proxy measure of cost. It is more realistic to think of cost as something that one would calculate, rather than measure in each case. It follows that one would require measures of the incidence and duration of exposure to the type or types of guidance under consideration. It would be a fairly simple matter to devise typologies of guidance interventions for this purpose, providing that one did not fall into the trap of over-description (although it is always tempting to introduce complications which one believes may help to distinguish the most from the least effective inputs, and hence to go down the path towards the examination of 'mechanisms'). The chief difficulty here would be obtaining valid data in non-experimental forms of investigation. For example, would young people accurately recall the extent of their exposure to careers education, delivered as part of personal and social education, and as an element of 'active tutorial' programmes? Once again, the problem lies less in knowing what one wants to know, than in determining how best to find out.

D. How to Measure the Economic Effects of Guidance

The task is to relate inputs (or guidance processes) to outcomes. Assuming with some confidence that each can be measured, what sort of strategy should one adopt? Plainly we need data which cover both inputs, and outcomes in education, training and the labour market, in conjunction. This implies longitudinal data, or cross-sectional data with a time structure (educational and work histories, for example).

The strategy also depends (crucially) on the scale of anticipated effects. For an economist, the aim might be to diminish a labour-market imperfection: that of imperfect information. An occupational psychologist might think in terms of an improved 'match' of individuals to jobs. These ideas are not very far apart, and in each case the underlying intention is to improve upon an existing state of affairs. Guidance does not inaugurate the flow of information, or 'matching'. Nor does guidance perfect these processes. In each case, one is seeking to improve upon what exists. One is therefore working towards an associated and equally modest improvement in economic criterion variables.

As we have been at pains to point out in Section Two, when costs and benefits (or costs and utilities) are considered together, even quite modest effects may be worth having. In Section Three, we had cause to complain that evaluators have often mounted investigations incapable of (confidently) demonstrating anything other than sizable ones. To detect modest differences reliably requires either very well-controlled experimental studies, or well-conducted studies with large samples. Experimental studies controlled to the necessary degree over the time period needed to get to 'economic' outcomes are hard to mount, for the reasons described in Section Three. Large sample studies are relatively feasible, but expensive.

These points make only too obvious some of the practical reasons that have inhibited the economic evaluation of guidance. Careers guidance, as a relatively small part of the labour-market scene, has lacked the resources to mount the kind of ambitious study which we are referring to. But there is an alternative road. This is to climb on board one or more of the major surveys of education, training or the labour market, which are already addressing the kinds of outcome measure likely to be of interest, and to add questions about guidance processes.

Examples of forthcoming studies which might offer potential are the Working Lives study being conducted by the Employment Department, the TVEI Evaluation Study, and evaluation of the Training Credits development. Addition of a longitudinal component to the Careers Service's study of attitudes towards careers guidance of 16–19-year-olds in education might also provide scope for economic evaluation of guidance effects. Any surveys of unemployment, or of unemployed groups such as Employment Training participants, would also be highly relevant.

It should also be said that the introduction of questioning about guidance processes would contribute towards an improvement in the conceptualisation and design of many labour-market surveys, and would contribute to better fulfilment of their existing purposes. For example, one of the weaknesses of existing surveys of unemployment has been their lack of detailed examination of the administrative and support processes which individuals have passed through. We know that people have visited Jobcentres, for instance, but we know little about what types of assistance they received. Questioning about guidance would begin to fill a void in the design of labour market surveys.

Large-sample surveys, as we have already mentioned, are needed to stand a good chance of demonstrating effects which are small (of the order, say, of a five per cent improvement in the outcome measure). Additional advantages of large-sample surveys, from the viewpoint of evaluating careers guidance, are offered by the scope they provide for using some advances in large-sample statistical techniques which have taken place in recent years. Among these two are particularly worthy of note.

First, there is a natural variation in the distribution of careers guidance: some get it and some do not – or some get it to a professional standard and others do not. But this distribution is unlikely to be random. The characteristics of individuals, and of their schools or other local institutions, are likely to bias chances of getting guidance, for or against. This means that we are dealing with non-random effects if we then seek to evaluate the outcome. At one time that would have meant that we could not get a rigorous answer, but that is no longer the case. If we can develop a good model of what distinguished the recipients from the non-recipients in the first place, we can then apply a variation of the now widely used incidental truncation, or sample selection, model, to analyse outcome data that are of this form. It would still be neater to have an experimental design with random allocation, but a non-experimental situation makes much less difference than it used to (for statistical discussion, see Greene, 1990).

The second advance is the development of statistical analysis methods which, so to speak, make a virtue out of sample structuring. A large survey is very likely to be based on a *selection* of travel-to-work-areas or TEC areas, local education authorities, or postal areas, and within these there may be a sampling of schools, Jobcentres, managing agents, or employer' establishments. Each of these units provides a natural sample cluster of the individuals to be surveyed; the tendency of surveys to use clusters is entirely to do with practicality and costs. However, if the clusters are inherently interesting – and all those listed above, with the exception of postal areas, probably are, from the viewpoint of guidance – then why not make the clustering units an integral part of the statistical analysis? We can then find out how much, for example, the differences in outcomes discovered in a survey are due to differences in local education authorities, or to differences in schools, rather than (or as well as) to differences in pupils or guidance provision. This is precisely what the technique of variance components analysis permits (for a recent example, see Smith and Tomlinson, 1989).

There are, then, some exciting possibilities for introducing the concerns expressed in this report into the design of forthcoming surveys. However, it should also not be forgotten that many surveys concerning education, training and labour markets were carried out in the 1980s, often considering issues in a way which at least made some contact with the concerns of guidance. These include, for example, surveys of unemployment, including many questions about job search and job advisory services; the Youth Cohort Surveys, which have included short items on receipt of guidance, in at least some sweeps; and surveys of choices and destinations when moving through various stages of the education system. Secondary analysis of these data may be a useful first step along the road.

E. Understanding the Mechanisms

It is quite possible for the external observer to adopt the position that, providing guidance generates benign effects, and providing that this is done efficiently, the manner in which it does so is a matter only for those directly involved. But if we wish to encourage evaluation *by* the guidance community (which contains few trained in research) then we need to provide it with the means and encouragement to do so. This implies taking a more-than-passing interest in guidance mechanisms, for reasons which we shall now try to make plain.

Everything we have said so far points to one conclusion. It will not be routinely possible for local guidance agencies to demonstrate their effectiveness against economic criteria. The task is simply too difficult, protracted and (from the perspective of a local provider) expensive. It is not difficult to count processes or inputs, and it is not *too* difficult to collect 'follow-up' data on at least some of the economic outcomes we have described, although even this may be beyond the capacity of the least well-resourced providers. But even if available, this information cannot of itself demonstrate effectiveness, for the reasons we have outlined in some detail. It follows that if guidance is to be evaluated on a routine local basis, and if innovation and development are to be encouraged, we need to find a way to link *real* effects which *can* be measured reasonably easily, to those (economic ones) which cannot. This brings us to what are sometimes called the 'outputs' of guidance.

Over several decades, a new conception has emerged of the 'mechanism' which links guidance to its economic outcomes. This corresponds to changes in practice and in the intended immediate effects which guidance has. It is important not be too dogmatic here. Recommendations are still made, and these are sometimes based upon the use of psychometric devices, linked to performance and satisfaction projections by occupational type. However, it is no longer possible to ignore the – at least equal and probably superior – claim that 'learning outcomes' now have over 'congruence' as the category of variables which are considered to mediate the effects of guidance (although 'social support' is also a widely-recognised mechanism deserving of attention). Two links in the evaluative chain already exist. We know that guidance does generate learning outcomes (Killeen and Kidd, 1991) and we know that some variables which have acted as learning outcome criteria, or are conceptually similar to them, are related to subsequent career and educational events.

This is not the place for an extended review of the latter but, for example, Kidd (1981) reports a small number of studies in which measures of vocational maturity have been shown to be significantly correlated with subsequent 'occupational and career satisfaction and success'[1]. Further evidence is available from studies which have considered variables *similar* to those employed as learning (and associated) outcomes, indicating effects on student drop-out, job offers and entry into employment[2]. The general implication of such studies is that information, the manner of decision-making and quality of decision, decidedness itself, the extent and character of job-search activities, and how information arising from job search is used – all of which are matters to which guidance addresses itself – are connected to 'economic' outcomes.

What we now need to do, therefore, is to join together these links in the chain, just as an earlier generation of investigators did for 'congruence'. Longitudinal studies are required which inspect the relationships between guidance, learning outcomes, and subsequent educational and career events.

If such studies were to take place, and if learning gains were shown to mediate the effect of guidance on economic outcomes, this would underwrite subsequent low-cost, routine, but technically adequate forms of evaluation against learning gains. Routine assessment of this kind would have the considerable advantage of being in line with what guidance practitioners say that they try to achieve. (A perhaps unwelcome bonus could be that if these linkages were not established, it would be necessary for the guidance community to revise its ideas about how guidance really works.)

In this case, secondary analysis of existing data-sets is not a realistic prospect. One can be fairly confident that appropriate data-sets do not exist. In any event, longitudinal rather than cross-sectional data would be required. It seems impractical, on the face of things, to suppose that one could intrude the measurement of learning outcomes into general labour-market surveys, but we do not rule this out. More to the point, it may be that the prominent mention given to guidance in association with a succession of initiatives, from TVEI to training credits, points to a concordance of interests between those who wish to evaluate guidance, and those concerned with the evaluation of more specific programmes. (At the end of the day, it might be necessary to consider mounting longitudinal studies devoted solely to the purpose now under consideration, but we are not sanguine about the feasibility of this course, for the reasons already given.)

What shape would studies of this kind take? One of the simplest kinds of study would be much as we have already described for the assessment of economic outcomes. It would, however, differ in one important respect.

It would be necessary to introduce measurement of learning outcome variables at appropriate stages. By means of the modelling techniques to which we have alluded, one would go on to inspect the intervening role of learning variables in any relationship between guidance inputs and economic outcomes. An extension of this strategy would involve deliberate and substantial enhancement of the guidance to which some sample members were exposed. For the reasons we have described elsewhere, it is unlikely that this could take a random-assigned controlled-trial form, which is why the modelling approach would continue to be so important. It is possible to point to initiatives such as training credits which might be susceptible to selective guidance enhancement on a trial basis, and in which such trials could be justified not only because one wishes to inspect the mechanisms of guidance in abstract, but because guidance is assumed to be important to their success.

These sorts of studies could, in turn, adopt two forms. In the simpler, one would test learning variables at suitable points in time, and inspect for associations with prior guidance inputs (and later economic outcomes). In the more complex, one would measure learning variables before and after exposure to particular guidance interventions amongst selected sub-samples. It is unrealistic to think that one could routinely do this for all of the guidance to which all members of a large sample were exposed. But direct testing of gains on a sub-sample basis would greatly increase confidence in the eventual results. In effect, one would be attempting to confirm in a direct way the inference from modelling that learning variables were influenced by guidance inputs, amongst sub-samples of those concerning whom the inference was made.

F. How Should We Measure Learning Outcomes?

If we come to understand rather better the mechanisms whereby guidance produces its ultimate effects, then we also come into possession of an invaluable tool of future evaluation. This is because it is much easier to investigate gains in immediately-intended effects (learning outcomes) than in remote ones. Moreover, in the interim we have to accept that guidance practitioners seek in the main to achieve learning gains. Thus in the shorter term, too, we need to measure the learning gains of routine practice, rather than merely assert that they occur because experimental studies have demonstrated them.

Learning outcome measurement takes us beyond 'process counting', without entailing the difficulties of full economic assessment. As a first step,

therefore, we need to devise measures of learning outcomes which fulfil the following criteria:
(i) They should go across the full range of outcomes for which existing evidence exists in experimental studies, most of which have been conducted in the United States. That is to say, they should include measures of precursors (attitudinal), self learning, opportunity awareness, decision-making skills, transition skills and decidedness.
(ii) They should be standardised, although distinct variants may be desirable for major guidance sub-populations.
(iii) They should be simple. Measures intended to make differing forms of intervention commensurate should not (and cannot) seek comprehensively to measure the details of learning in any one case. The task of measuring learning outcomes as performance indicators should be kept distinct from that of full learning assessment.

In the interests of standardisation, simplicity and parsimony, consideration should be given to the use of subjective measures of perceived knowledge and skill gain. The usual arguments against subjective measures would not apply if the criteria listed above were met and if, during the instrument development phase, (successful) comparisons were made between these brief subjective measures, and objectives ones designed for the purpose of their validation.

If one were to attempt to devise a very detailed instrument for widespread application, then one would, arguably, be heading towards spectacular failure. It is extremely important to preserve a distinction between measures capable of indicating the amount of learning which has occurred, and more detailed devices. No attempt has been made to develop a simple device for the purpose of guidance assessment. In the United States, the Attitude Scale of Crites' Career Maturity Inventory (CMI:AS) has come to play this role, in the sense that it is employed in a larger number of guidance experiments than any other, and thus makes a proportion of studies commensurate. This is, however, only by default. The device was not devised with this purpose in view, it does not pretend to assess the full range of learning of concern to us, and we do not know how it is related either to other kinds of learning, or to economic effects. A need plainly exists to fix upon a more considered UK alternative which answers to the requirements we have listed. But there is no virtue in reinventing the wheel. Our first task should be to inspect existing devices, almost all of which are American in origin, in order to determine how well they meet these requirements.

This, then, is how we believe we might best proceed.

Notes

Section One
1. Distinguishing 'formal' from 'informal' channels and types of guidance has led to much confusion. Usages tend to be taken-over from the classification of job placement channels. The chief ambiguities arise from the treatment of formal channels as either public sector (e.g. Risk, 1987) or 'publicly available' (Raffe, 1985).

Section Three
1. For statistical readers, Effect Size (ES) was usually calculated as delta (Glass *et al.*, 1981)

   $$ES = \frac{Me - Mc}{SDc}$$

   These were post-test measures (see note 2). Alternative methods were used in the absence of means/standard deviations (Glass *et al.*, 1981; Smith *et al.*, 1980). In the case of multiple outcomes, mean study effect sizes were calculated (non-independence issue). Mean effect size across all studies was calculated with and without deletion of outliers, with and without the inclusion of one large sample study having a null result, and with and without weighting by sample size. Exclusion of the single large sample study had trivial consequences (increase in upper ES estimate of 0.02) and is set aside. On the other bases, mean ES was in the range 0.39 to 0.82. This equates to a percentile improvement by the average experimental subject in the range 15 to 29 percentile points.
2. In the absence of a control group: see note 4 below. In practice, non-controlled pre/post-test studies are less frequent than controlled ones, which we discuss separately. In the simplest form of controlled trial, comparisons are made between experimental and control groups only at the 'post-test' stage. The control group mean score on any given outcome is taken to represent what the experimental group mean

would have been, if it had not been exposed to the guidance intervention. When timescales are very short, this is often thought to approximate to what the experimental group mean really was, prior to the intervention. However, it should be clear that this is not necessarily true. For example, a decline occurring in the control group could have been arrested in the experimental group.
3. This showed the main gains to be in 'awareness of option scope' and 'planning for implementation'.
4. This is because of what experimentalists call 'history' and 'maturation'. That is, the possibility exists that external factors other than guidance, or unrelated developments in the individual, might be responsible for apparent effects. We can add a related consideration. Formal guidance may provide the means for things to happen which would occur through other means if guidance were not offered. These alternative means may be contemporaneously available. They may, however, be historically conditioned. Trials with control groups allow us to examine the effect size of guidance against all but the last-mentioned historical possibility. To do this is to correct for what economists call 'deadweight'. But formal guidance may, somewhat abstractly, be thought to have functional substitutes (with regard to its economic effects) which would emerge, if guidance ceased to exist. We must accept this limitation. Experimental methods examine relationships in their historical context, and we shall not be concerned to challenge that context here. Moreover, where trials involve small samples, we may be reasonably confident that what economists call 'substitution' and 'displacement' effects do not occur: that is, that Peter is not robbed to pay Paul. But where experiments become large-scale interventions, one must, of course, go on to envisage the possibility that they distribute rather than create gains. This is a further limitation which must be accepted here.
5. This family is very extensive, but most of its members go unrepresented in guidance research. For example, in studies of learning outcomes, where instrument reactivity can be a problem, the pre/post-test design continues to predominate. This design does not allow us to distinguish instrument reactivity from history and maturation. More complex designs, such as the Solomon four-group design, can cope with this problem. However, despite the fact that designs other than those conventionally adopted are sometimes advocated, they are seldom adopted.
6. It is often thought that random assignment ensures that experimental and control groups are 'the same'. Thus in post-test only designs, mean

differences between experimental and control groups provide a measure of the effect of guidance (see note 1). The logic of this design is simple. Significant differences between randomly drawn samples are attributed to events occurring after the samples were drawn. As the matched pairs strategy implies, however, random assignment does not equalise samples. To assume the contrary is to ignore sampling error. But as should be plain, where sample assignment is genuinely random, the balance of probabilities remains in favour of the experimental effect being genuine. As the number of measured outcomes in any study increases, so does the probability that significant differences will be fortuitously found. Replication is thus desirable since it has the potential greatly to increase our confidence that the results of any initial study are not fortuitous.
7. The 'Job-Club' is a well-described assembly of activities based on a group-support strategy. The results reported by Azrin and his collaborators refer to that strategy and not to other interventions to which the name 'Job Club' is sometimes casually applied. The UK intervention for *individuals* studied by Davison (1986) has, for example, been called an 'abbreviated Job Club'.
8. Congruence designs are an inadequate test of conditional predictions of the kind 'If A enters occupation B, then (s)he will benefit more than if (s)he enters occupations NOT B'. The comparison should be between two possible futures for A (B and NOT B), only one of which occurs. But this comparison is impossible for the job entered after guidance. By definition, only one of the 'alternative futures' has occurred. Thus if congruent groups benefit more, on average, than incongruent ones, this is a necessary but insufficient condition for the prediction to have been true of the average case. The test actually made is of a corollary, not of the prediction itself. Longitudinal studies, which are able to relate outcome variables to the movement of individuals between congruent and incongruent jobs, ameliorate to some degree this problem of unobserved 'alternative futures'. Studies by Earle (1931) and Hunt and Smith (1944) both showed that movement towards congruence in experimental samples was globally associated with rising levels of satisfaction. But there are all sorts of reasons why benefits could be greater on average in the congruent group. The key one, in the sense that it undermines the conditional (if) prediction directly, is the possibility that 'congruent' people differ from 'incongruent' ones in ways related to subsequent benefits but unrelated to

job entered. Moreover, by acting at variance with the spirit but not the wording of the prediction, one could generate rewards to congruence by always recommending 'good jobs'. (But we have to be careful with the 'good jobs' hypothesis. This is because guidance may be intended to increase human capital investment and to allow individuals to maximise the utilisation of their abilities, and thus to enter 'better' jobs. A tendency has existed to treat entry into the labour-market as a zero-sum game. This implies that gains by one individual are associated with losses by another. Such an approach simply ignores the possibility of supply-side effects on the industrial and occupational structure.) More complex possibilities exist. If, for example, the apparent effect size of congruence is related to the ratio of congruent and incongruent cases, it is easy to imagine feedback and learning mechanisms which lead to its inductive maximisation, not merely in evaluation studies (where critics will be alert to the possibility), but also in the practice of guidance itself, by adjustment of the level of occupational aggregation entailed in recommendations. Moreover, if occupational recommendations are more or less specific in ways related to known occupational distributions of satisfaction, etc., this effect could be magnified. In addition, occupations have differential entry rates, not necessarily taken into account in recommendations. The second major difficulty is that even if the predictions made by 'expert matching' guidance are true, it does not follow that such guidance is effective. From the point of view of public policy, the overall effect of guidance on its clients, rather than upon (possibly small) sub-groups is a matter of obvious importance. But the even starker possibility exists that such guidance might predict without exercising influence. Earle (1931), for example, opined that only 1% of his experimental group had been 'influenced' by guidance recommendations, so it is not at all clear that one should characterise congruence as 'following a recommendation'. Guidance recommendations may simply anticipate certain aspects of employers' decision-making which, in turn, determine the distribution of rewards. They may be influenced by rather than influence the intentions and preferences of clients, and thus congruence may indicate the realisation of intentions, and the benefits deriving therefrom (although self-referring clients may reasonably be supposed to be undecided). Accordingly, pure congruence designs, without control comparisons and/or a multivariate element, always beg questions.

9. Other reasons include sampling error, contamination by factors associated with but not part of the guidance intervention, and failure of randomly assigned experimental and control groups to be representative of the population to which extrapolation is made (external validity).
10. Hill employed multinomial logit models in an attempt to disentangle the effects of interventions for the visually disabled. The models were based upon administratively available data for a large sample (n=17,228) of successfully rehabilitated individuals. Two (undescribed) constituent services ('diagnosis' and 'restorative') apparently refer to the counselling, as opposed to training elements of interventions. They occur only as binary variables (present; not present): 95% of sample members received 'diagnosis', and 57% the 'restorative' service. This is, therefore, an extremely crude analysis – sample size and modelling technique notwithstanding. In comparison with clients' age, sex, prior education, degree of disablement and other training interventions, the effects of the counselling interventions on entry into open employment, self-employment and sheltered work (each in comparison to placement as a 'homemaker') are small. But unfortunately, whereas two modest but apparently *negative* effects are shown in a table of results (table 2, p.227), textual reference is made only to one of them, as a *positive* effect: 'Restorative services increased the likelihood of placement in sheltered work relative to being placed as a homemaker' (p.228).
11. In the US, 'Comprehensive Employment and Training Programs' (CETA) have been evaluated against an operational definition of 'successful placement' highlighted in Figure 2, together with measures of subjective satisfaction.
12. These studies are subject to the accusation of potential bias resulting from non-response, although Handyside and Stott (1958) made an elaborate attempt to counter this possibility, by comparing respondent profiles to the population parameters: the profiles of all of those exposed to guidance.
13. As already observed of Burt *et al.*'s (1926) study, the disparity between congruent and non-congruent group outcomes, or the apparent influence of congruence on job retention, satisfaction, etc., would probably have been greater in Earle's study if those in occupations 'judged similar' to recommendations had been classified as 'congruent'. This rests on an important general hypothesis: that in two-category

(congruent, not congruent) comparisons, the difference between mean congruent and non-congruent outcome scores is related to the proportion of all cases classified as congruent. There are, however, other important differences between the studies in question. At the end of his 2.5 to 4 year follow-up (dependent upon date of school leaving) of 1,200 London school leavers, Earle achieved an 82.5% response rate. Hunt and Smith's first Birmingham study achieved a similar rate (85.7%) over a somewhat shorter period (2.5 to 3 years), but against a modest initial sample (328). Their later study, which was in essence a large-scale replication (n=3,000), suffered much greater attrition, to 54.6% at two years and 20.1% at four years. In addition, whereas in each study comparisons were made on the basis of congruence of first and subsequent posts, many of Earle's main comparisons were based on the last post held or on 'all posts'. Earle also employed average congruence ratings.

14. Earle found less initial congruence with scientific guidance recommendations than conventional ones. In both of their studies, Hunt (Allen) and Smith found the reverse. All found congruence with conventional recommendations to decline over time, but only Hunt and Smith found congruence with scientific guidance recommendation to increase. Precise results were as follows. *Earle (1931)*. Initial congruence: Experimental Group 21%; Control Group 34%. Congruence at end of trial period (last known post): Experimental Group 19.6%; Control Group 21%. Note also that for last known post, the distribution of classifiable jobs on a five-point congruence scale was nearly identical between groups. On a more 'relaxed' definition of congruence (top two congruence ratings), this was 46% in both groups. *Allen and Smith (1932)*. Initial congruence: Experimental Group 61%; Control Group 41%. *Hunt and Smith (1944)*. Initial congruence: Experimental Group 77%; Control Group 64%. At four years: Experimental Group 92%; Control Group 47%. But note attrition of sample to 20.1% of original.
15. Earle (1931) measured 'liking' coded *post hoc* from qualitative date. Allen and Smith (1932) measured job satisfaction in a similar way, but with a higher effective non-response due to the 'vague' character of many children's 'remarks'. Later, Hunt and Smith (1944) adopted a standardised self-report measure of 'job suitability'. These differences also militate against comparison between studies.
16. 54% of those entering such jobs, compared to 34% in the control group.

17. The 'approve/disapprove' distinction is crude, and many young people change their intentions. Thus a high degree of accuracy is unlikely in a static study such as this. As is also true of the studies which follow, Sillitoe and Meltzer did not attempt to capture the dynamics of the relationship between young people and the Careers Service.
18. Selection criteria not given.
19. Cherry measured concordance (and other agreements) by coding recommendations, intentions and outcomes in a 4-level/12-category matrix, the latter being based upon the occupational categories of the Rothwell-Miller Interest Blank. She found that 'concordant' jobs were better matched to measured ability and measured interests (RMIB) than were 'discordant' ones: *prima facie* evidence for the rationality of YEO recommendations, and for improvement in the quality of service, when compared to that offered by pre-war Juvenile Employment Officers in the studies conducted by Allen/Hunt and Smith. Poor matching and discordance disposed both boys and girls to early job leaving (defined as one or more moves within six months of entry to first job).
20. There was, however, an interactive relationship with sex and type of discordance. For boys, discordance with YEO recommendations as to *level* of occupation was somewhat more likely to be followed by early job leaving than discordance *exclusively* by *type* of occupation. For girls, this pattern was reversed.
21. Effects interact with sex. But numerous other methodological differences exist (e.g. the ways in which data were gathered; procedures for judging concordance; and the time period over which job movement was recorded – six months by Cherry, but eighteen months by Thomas).
22. Some guidance agencies, such as the Careers Service, actively target special groups, such as ex-offenders, those with special training needs, etc., who may be regarded as possessing weak labour-market characteristics. This is as part of their more general provision.
23. There is evidence both of heightened levels of aspiration amongst members of ethnic minorities, and of relative underestimation of their ability by COs (Sillitoe and Meltzer, 1985; Cross *et al.*, 1990). COs' recommendations may also anticipate employer discrimination.
24. A cut-off date was used to classify subjects, and thus is a crude indicator of job-search duration. Data are not fully reported, but the interpretation given here seems the most appropriate one.

25. See note 7.
26. Realistic job previews are an attempt by employers to provide adequate information to potential recruits. 'Surprise' is a feature of entry to employment (Mabey, 1986), whereas confirmation of expectations exercises an early influence on organisational commitment (Meyer and Allen, 1988). Commitment is related to turnover (Porter *et al.*, 1974). Thus realistic job previews may reduce turnover. Meta-analyses of US research (Guzzo *et al.*, 1985; McEvoy and Cascio, 1985; Premack and Wanous, 1985) are equivocal. Guzzo *et al.* found no effect on turnover, whereas the two other studies found small effects. Turning to employee counselling, most US evidence relates to personal counselling (inclusive of debt counselling, etc.) of a kind beyond our current concern. Although career development counselling occurs and is intended, amongst other things, to diminish employee out-flows, studies are descriptive, and claims concerning reduced turnover are usually unsubstantiated (e.g. Papalia and Kaminsky, 1981).
27. In Earle's (1931) study, the mean numbers of jobs held were: Experimental Group 2.98, Control Group 3.33. Hunt and Smith's results were: at two years, Experimental Group 2.0, Control Group 2.26; at four years, Experimental Group 2.42, Control Group 2.77.
28. West and Newton (1982) included participation in training amongst the outcomes they studied. Ostensibly they compared the relative effectiveness of two forms of careers education and guidance. Actually they compared the experience of leavers from two schools which differed markedly in many other ways. Further inadequacies are demonstrated in UK evaluations of computer aided careers guidance systems (CACGS). The National Council for Educational Technology (1988) conducted trials of a number of such systems (for possible incorporation to Training Access Points). As part of this study, a very small sample (n=83) follow-up to users occurred. This indicated that 'very few' went on to enrol in education or training. However, these results were not quantified and no other details of the study, such as sample construction, are given. An NFER study of JIIG-CAL (1987) looked at its impact on option choices and 'wastage' (subsequent option changing). The deficiencies of this study have already been described (p.57). Closs *et al.*'s study of JIIG-CAL considered satisfaction with subsequent education and training. This study is not fully described, and troublesome inconsistencies are displayed in the recording of sample numbers. Over a three-year period experimental subjects

apparently increased from 1,223 to 1,815 subjects, whereas controls declined from 1,760 to 583. Percentage reporting of results makes it difficult to see what the true numbers were. We have criticised the congruence element of this study elsewhere. Reed and Bazalgette's (1983) report of the impact of a specialised form of transition to work and adult life course on voluntary attendance is ambiguously and incompletely reported.
29. A non-random *post hoc* matched-pairs trial. This is often the best that can be achieved, and raises the issue of 'motivation'. Some US studies have, however, used 'motivated controls' (see Campbell, 1965).
30. 28% of the jobs held by the group exposed to scientific guidance were 'unsuitable'; only marginally more, 31%, were so for the controls.
31. One UK study of unemployed job seekers exists which failed to demonstrate a congruence effect (Butler *et al.*, 1972). The sample was, however, very small (n=100).

Section Four
1. These include 'planfulness', 'occupational information', 'interest maturity', and 'crystallisation of interests' (Super *et al.*, 1967; Jordaan and Super, 1974), CMI-AS (Career Maturity Inventory Attitude Scale) (Cox: quoted in Crites, 1973) and several 'Readiness for Vocational Planning' subscales (Gribbons and Lohnes, 1968).
2. Titley and Titley (1980) investigated 'decidedness' and undergraduate drop-out, finding an inverse relationship. In addition, the probability and number of job offers and/or entry into employment have been associated with 'crystallised specific goals' and 'independent active search' (Stevens, 1986), the pursuit of 'specific job ideas' by the unemployed (Daniel, 1990) and 'occupational knowledge' and 'self awareness' (interests, abilities) prior to search (Taylor, 1985).

References

Allen, E.P., and Smith, P.: *The Value of Vocational Tests as Aids to Choice of Employment: Report of Research.* Birmingham: City of Birmingham Education Committee, 1932.

Alloway, J: *Advice and Guidance to Individuals.* Leicester: Unit for the Development of Adult Continuing Education, 1986.

Amatea, E.S., Clark, J.E., and Cross, E.G.: 'Life Styles: Evaluating a Life-Role Planning Program for High-School Students'. *Vocational Guidance Quarterly*, Vol.32 No.4, 1984 pp. 249–259.

Amundson, N.E., and Borgen, W.A.: 'Factors that Help and Hinder in Group Employment Counseling'. *Journal of Employment Counseling*, Vol.25 No.3, 1988, pp. 104–114.

Arbeiter, S., Aslanian, C.B., Schonerbeck, F.A., and Brickell, H.M.: *40 Million Americans in Career Transition.* New York: College Entrance Examinations Board, 1978.

Azrin, N.H., Flores, T., and Kaplan, S.J.: 'Job-Finding Club: a Group Assisted Program for Obtaining Employment'. *Behavior Research and Therapy*, Vol.13, 1975, pp. 17–27.

Azrin, N.H., Philip, R.A., Thienes-Hontos, P., and Besalel, V.A.: 'Comparative Evaluation of the Job Club Program with Welfare Recipients'. *Journal of Vocational Behavior*, Vol.16, 1980, pp. 133–145.

Azrin, N.H., Philip, R.A., Thienes-Hontos, P., and Besalel, V.A.: 'Follow-Up on Welfare Benefits Received by Job Club Clients'. *Journal of Vocational Behavior*, Vol.18, 1981, pp. 253–254.

Ball, C.: *Learning Pays: Interim Report.* London: Royal Society for the Encouragement of Arts, Manufactures and Commerce, 1991.

Becker, G.S.: *Human Capital* (2nd ed.). New York: National Bureau of Economic Research, 1975.

Bedford, T.: *Vocational Guidance Interviews: a Survey by the Careers Service Inspectorate.* London: Careers Service Branch, Department of Employment, 1982.

Best, F.: *Exchanging Earnings for Leisure: Findings of an Exploratory National Survey on Work-Time Preferences.* Research and Development

Monograph No.79. Washington DC: United States Department of Labor, 1980.
Boys, C.J., and Kirkland, J.: *Degrees of Success*. London: Jessica Kingsley, 1988.
Breen, R.: *Education and the Labour Market: Work and Unemployment among Recent Cohorts of Irish School Leavers*. Paper No.119. Dublin: Economic and Social Research Institute, 1984.
Brown, W.F.: 'Student-to-Student Counseling for Academic Adjustment'. *Personnel and Guidance Journal*, Vol.53, 1965, pp. 811–817.
Burt, C., Gaw, F., Ramsey, L., Smith, M., and Spielman, W.: *A Study in Vocational Guidance*. MRC Industrial Fatigue Research Board Report No.33. London: HMSO, 1926.
Busshoff, L., and Heller, K.A.: 'Educational and Vocational Guidance Services for the 14–25 Age-Group in the Federal Republic of Germany'. In Watts, A.G., Dartois, C., and Plant, P. (eds.): *Educational and Vocational Guidance Services for the 14–25 Age-Group: Denmark, Federal Republic of Germany and the Netherlands*. Luxembourg: Office for Official Institutions of the European Communities, 1988.
Butler, F.J.J., Crinnion, J., and Martin, J.: 'The Kuder Preference Record in Adult Vocational Guidance'. *Journal of Occupational Psychology*, Vol.46, 1972, pp. 99–104.
Cairo, P.C.: 'Counseling in Industry: a Selected Review of the Literature'. *Personnel Psychology*, Vol.36, 1983, pp. 1–18.
Campbell, D.P.: *The Results of Counseling: Twenty-Five Years Later*. Philadelphia: Saunders, 1965.
Chandler, A.L.: 'Using an Abbreviated Job Club Programme in a Job Service Setting'. *Journal of Employment Counseling*, Vol.21 No.3, 1984, pp. 98–102.
Cherry, N.: 'Do Careers Officers Give Good Advice?' *British Journal of Guidance and Counselling*, Vol.2, 1974, pp. 27–40.
Cherry, N.: 'Choosing a First Job'. In Cherry, N., Douglas, J., Nelson, J., Atkins, E., and Lowe, M.: *Young School Leavers at Work and College*. London: National Survey of Health and Development. 1, 1971 (mimeo).
Closs, S.J., Maclean, P.R., and Walker, M.V.: *An Evaluation of the JIIG-CAL System*. Sevenoaks: Hodder & Stoughton, 1985 (mimeo).
Confederation of British Industry: *Towards a Skills Revolution*. Report of the Vocational Education and Training Task Force. London: CBI, 1990.

References

Crites, J.O.: *Career Maturity Inventory: Theory and Research Handbook*. Monterey, California: California Test Bureau/McGraw-Hill, 1973.

Crites, J.O.: 'The Career Maturity Inventory'. In Super, D.E. (ed.): *Measuring Vocational Maturity for Counseling and Evaluation*. Washington, DC: National Vocational Guidance Association, 1974.

Cross, M., Wrench, J., and Barnett, S.: *Ethnic Minorities and the Careers Service: an Investigation into Processes of Assessment and Placement*. Department of Employment Research Paper No.73. London: Department of Employment, 1990.

Crowley-Bainton, T., and White, M.: *Employing Unemployed People: How Employers Gain*. Sheffield: Employment Service, 1990.

Daniel, W.W.: *The Unemployed Flow*. London: Policy Studies Institute, 1990.

Davison: *TARGET: a Structured Approach to LTV Caseload*. Psychological Services Regional Report. London: Manpower Services Commission, 1986. (Cited in Carroll, P.: *The Potential of Guidance for Making Job Search More Effective*. ES Research and Evaluation Branch Report No.27. London: Manpower Services Commission, 1987.)

Department of Education and Science/Department of Employment: *Education and Training for the 21st Century*, Volume 1. London: HMSO, 1991.

Department of Employment: '1988 Labour Force Survey – Preliminary Results'. *Employment Gazette*, April 1989(a).

Department of Employment: 'Measures of Unemployment: Claimant Count and Labour Force Survey'. *Employment Gazette*, August 1989(b).

Dex, S: 'Job Search Methods and Ethnic Discrimination'. *New Community*, Vol.7 No.1, Winter 1978, pp.31–39.

Earle, F.M.: *Methods of Choosing a Career*. London: Harrap, 1931.

Fairbairns, J. and Coolbear, J.: *Career Development Counselling: an Experiment*. Sheffield: Manpower Services Commission, 1982.

Farid-Uddin, D.H.I.S.: *A Thirty-Year Vocational Guidance Follow-Up Study*. PhD thesis, University of London, 1971.

Fretz, B.R.: 'Evaluating the Effectiveness of Career Interventions'. *Journal of Counseling Psychology Monograph*, Vol.28, 1981, pp. 77–90.

Full Employment UK: *Investing in Skills: Part Four*. London: Full Employment UK, 1991 (mimeo).

Gambetta, D.: *Were They Pushed or Did They Jump?* Cambridge: Cambridge University Press, 1987.

Glass, G.V., McCraw, B., and Smith, M.L.: *Meta-Analysis in Social Research*. Beverly Hills, California: Sage, 1981.

Goldman, G.: 'Career Decision-Making and Interview Frequency'. *British Journal of Guidance and Counselling*, Vol.4 No.2, 1976, pp. 195–201.

Gottfredson, L.S.: 'Circumscription and Compromise: a Developmental Theory of Occupational Aspirations'. *Journal of Counseling Psychology*, Vol.28 No.6, 1981, pp. 545–579.

Greene, W.H.: *Econometric Analysis*. London: Collier-Macmillan, 1990.

Gribbons, W.D., and Lohnes, P.R.: *Emerging Careers*. New York: Teachers College Press, 1968.

Guzzo, R.A., Jette, R.D., and Katzell, R.A.: 'The Effects of Psychologically Based Intervention Programs on Worker Productivity: a Meta-Analysis'. *Personnel Psychology*, Vol.38, 1985, pp. 275–291.

Halsey, A.H., Heath, A.F., and Ridge, J.M.: *Origins and Destinations: Family, Class and Education in Modern Britain*. Oxford: Oxford University Press, 1980.

Hamandi, A.: 'Facilitating Vocational Development among Disadvantaged Inner-City Adolescents'. *Vocational Guidance Quarterly*, Vol.26, 1977, pp. 60–67.

Hamilton, J.A., and Mitchell, A.M.: 'Programs that Worked'. *Journal of Career Education*, Vol.5 No.4, 1979, pp. 243–249.

Handyside, J., and Stott, M.B.: 'The Effectiveness of Vocational Guidance'. *Medical World*, Vol.89, 1958, pp. 369–374.

Hannan, D., Hövels, B., van den Berg, S., and White, M.: 'Early Leavers from Education and Training in Ireland, the Netherlands, and the United Kingdom'. Paper presented under the EC PETRA programme at a workshop on 'Early Leavers from Education and Training', London, 1991.

Hesse, C.H.: 'PEP: an Enabling Program for CETA-Zen Employment'. *Personnel and Guidance Journal*, Vol.61 No.3, 1982, pp. 159–162.

Hill, M.A.: 'Work Status Outcomes of Vocational Rehabilitation Clients who are Blind or Visually Impaired'. *Rehabilitation Counseling Bulletin*, Vol.32, 1989, pp. 219–230.

Hopson, B.: 'The Effectiveness of a Careers Course in a Secondary School'. Vocational Guidance Research Unit, University of Leeds, 1970 (mimeo).

Horton, C.: *The Training and Development of Trainers*. Sheffield: Training Agency, 1990.

Hunt, E.P., and Smith, P.: *Scientific Vocational Guidance and its Value to the Choice of Employment Work of a Local Education Authority*. Birmingham: City of Birmingham Education Committee, 1944.

Iaffaldano, M.T., and Muchinsky, P.M.: 'Job Satisfaction and Job Performance: a Meta-Analysis'. *Psychological Bulletin*, Vol.97, 1985, pp. 251–273.

References

Ives, R.: 'Careers Advice and Obtaining a Job'. *Careers Journal*, Vol.5 No.3, 1985, pp. 33–36.

Jackman, R., Layard, R., and Savouri, S.: *Labour Market Mismatch: a Framework for Thought*. Discussion Paper No.1. London: Centre for Economic Performance, 1990.

Jennings, J.R., and Stott, M.B.: 'A Fourth Follow-Up of Vocationally Advised Cases (1930–1)'. *Human Factor*, Vol.X, 1936, pp. 165–174.

Joll, C., McKenna, C., McNabb, R., and Shorey, J.: *Developments in Labour Market Analysis*. London: Allen & Unwin, 1983.

Jolly, J., Creigh, S., and Mingay, A.: *Age as a Factor in Employment*. Research Paper No.11. London: Department of Employment, 1980.

Jordaan, J.P., and Super, D.E.: 'The Prediction of Early Adult Vocational Behavior'. In Ricks, D.F., Thomas, A., and Roff, M. (eds.): *Life History Research in Psychopathology, Vol.3*. Minneapolis: University of Minnesota Press, 1974.

Kidd, J.M.: 'The Assessment of Career Development'. In Watts, A.G., Super, D.E., and Kidd, J.M. (eds.): *Career Development in Britain*. Cambridge: CRAC/Hobsons, 1981.

Killeen, J.: 'Vocational Guidance for Adults: a Study of Demand'. *British Journal of Guidance and Counselling*, Vol.14 No.3, 1986, pp. 225–239.

Killeen, J., and Kidd, J.: *Learning Outcomes of Guidance: a Review of Recent Research*. Department of Employment Research Paper No.85. London: Department of Employment, 1991.

Koller, M., Reyher, L., and Teriet, B.: 'Le Travail à Temps Partiel en République Féderale d'Allemagne'. In Jallade, J.-P. (ed.): *L'Europe à Temps Partiel*. Paris: Economica, 1982.

Lancashire, R.: 'Changing Needs in Vocational Guidance Follow-Up'. Paper presented to Annual Conference of the British Psychological Society, 1971 (mimeo).

Law, B., and Watts, A.G.: *Schools, Careers and Community*. London: Church Information Office, 1977.

Lee, G., and Wrench, J.: *Skill Seekers: Black Youth, Apprenticeships and Disadvantage*. Leicester: National Youth Bureau, 1983.

Mabey, C.: *Graduates into Industry*. Aldershot, Hants.: Gower, 1986.

McEvoy, G.M., and Cascio, W.F.: 'Strategies for Reducing Employee Turnover'. *Journal of Applied Psychology*, Vol.70, 1985, pp. 342–353.

Macrae, A.: 'A Second Follow-Up of Vocationally Advised Cases (1927–8)'. *Human Factor*, Vol.VI, 1932, pp. 42–52.

Macrae, A.: 'A Third Follow-Up of Vocationally Advised Cases (1929)'. *Human Factor*, Vol.VII, 1933, pp. 41–50.

McLoughlin, E., Millar, J., and Cooke, K.: *Work and Welfare Benefits*. London: Avebury, 1989.

Narendranathan, W., and Nickell, S.: 'Modelling the Process of Job Search'. In Nickell, S., Narendranathan, W., Stern, J., and Garcia, J.: *The Nature of Unemployment in Britain*. Oxford: Oxford University Press, 1989.

National Council for Educational Technology: *Computer Aided Guidance Evaluation: an Evaluation of the Place of Computer Aided Guidance in the TAP Context and Evaluation of Specific Packages Trialled*. London: NCET, 1988 (mimeo).

National Foundation for Educational Research: *Job Ideas and Information Generator: Computer Assisted Learning (JIIG-CAL): Evaluation Report*. Slough: NFER, 1987 (mimeo).

Nelson-Jones, R., and Toner, H.L.: 'Assistance with Learning Competence and Decision-Making in Schools and Further Education'. *British Journal of Guidance and Counselling*, Vol.6 No.2, 1978, pp. 183–190.

Office of Population Censuses and Surveys: *The General Household Survey*. London: HMSO, 1989.

Organisation for Economic Cooperation and Development: *Economies in Transition: Structural Adjustment in OECD Countries*. Paris: OECD, 1989.

Oliver, L.W., and Spokane, A.R.: 'Career Intervention Outcome: What Contributes to Client Gain?' *Journal of Counseling Psychology*, Vol.35, 1988, pp. 447–462.

Papalia, A.S., and Kaminsky, W.: 'Counseling and Counseling Skills in the Industrial Environment'. *Vocational Guidance Quarterly*, Vol.60, 1981, pp. 37–42.

Pearson, R.W.: 'Creating Flexible Careers: Some Observations on a "Bridge" Programme for Unemployed Professionals'. *British Journal of Guidance and Counselling*, Vol.16 No.3, September 1988, pp. 250–267.

Petty, M.M., McGee, G.W., and Cavender, J.W.: 'A Meta-Analysis of the Relationships between Individual Job Satisfaction and Individual Performance'. *Academy of Management Review*, Vol.9, 1984, pp. 719–721.

Pickering, J.W., and Vacc, N.A.: 'Effectiveness of Career Development Interventions for College Students: a Review of Published Research'. *Vocational Guidance Quarterly*, Vol.32, 1984, pp. 149–159.

Porter, L.W., Crampon, W.J., and Smith, F.J.: 'Organizational Commitment and Managerial Turnover: a Longitudinal Study'. *Organizational Behavior and Human Performance*, Vol.15, 1974, pp. 87–98. (Cited in

References

Meyer, J.P., and Allen, N.J.: 'Links between Work Experiences and Organizational Commitment During the First Year of Employment: a Longitudinal Analysis'. *Journal of Occupational Psychology*, Vol.61, 1988, pp. 195–209.)

Premack, S.J., and Wanous, J.P.: 'A Meta-Analysis of Realistic Job Preview Experiments'. *Journal of Applied Psychology*, Vol.70, 1985, pp. 706–719.

Pryor, R.G.L.: 'Eradicating Sex-Role Stereotypes: an Application of Gottfredson's Circumscription-Compromise Theory'. *Vocational Guidance Quarterly*, Vol.33, 1985, pp. 277–283.

Pumfrey, P.D., and Schofield, A.: 'Work Experience and the Career Maturity of Fifth-Form Pupils'. *British Journal of Guidance and Counselling*, Vol.10 No.2, 1982, pp. 167–175.

Raffe, D.: 'Degrees of Informality: Methods of Job Placement among Scottish School-Leavers'. *British Journal of Guidance and Counselling*, Vol.13 No.3, September 1985, pp. 292–307.

Reed, B., and Bazalgette, J.: 'TWL Network and Schools'. In Watts, A.G. (ed.): *Work Experience and Schools*. London: Heinemann, 1983.

Risk, J.W.F.: 'The Recruitment Process for School-Leavers: Practical and Theoretical Implications'. *British Journal of Guidance and Counselling*, Vol.15 No.3, September 1987, pp. 297–312.

Rodenstein, J.M.: 'Follow-Up and Evaluation of Job Placement in Employment and Training'. *Journal of Employment Counseling*, Vol.19 No.4, 1982, pp. 171–183.

Rose, R., and Wignanek, G.: *Training without Trainers? How Germany Avoids Britain's Supply-Side Bottleneck*. London: Anglo–German Foundation, 1990.

Russell, J.E.A.: 'Career Development Interventions in Organizations'. *Journal of Vocational Behavior*, Vol.38 No.3, 1991, pp. 237–287.

Schlossberg, N.K., and Leibowitz, Z.: 'Organizational Support Systems as Buffers to Job Loss'. *Journal of Vocational Behavior*, Vol.17, 1980, pp. 204–217.

Sillitoe, K., and Meltzer, H.: *The West Indian School Leaver*, Vols.1 and 2. London: HMSO, 1985.

Smith, A.: *An Enquiry into the Nature and Causes of the Wealth of Nations*. Edinburgh: Black, 1776.

Smith, C.S.: 'Entry, Location and Commitment of Young Workers in the Labour Force: a Review of Sociological Thinking'. In Brannen, P. (ed.): *Entering the World of Work: Some Sociological Perspectives*. London: HMSO, 1978.

Smith, D.J., and Tomlinson, S.: *The School Effect*. London: Policy Studies Institute, 1989.

Smith, M.L., Glass, G.V., and Miller, T.I.: *The Benefits of Psychotherapy*. Baltimore, MD: Johns Hopkins University Press, 1980.

Spokane, A.R., and Oliver, L.W.: 'The Outcomes of Vocational Intervention'. In Walsh, W.B., and Osipow, S. H. (eds.): *Handbook of Vocational Psychology*, Vol.2. New Jersey: Erlbaum, 1983.

Standing Conference of Associations for Guidance in Educational Settings: 'Statement of Principles and Definitions'. Stourbridge: SCAGES, 1991 (mimeo).

Stevens, N.D.: *Dynamics of Jobseeking Behaviour*. Springfield, Illinois: C.C. Thomas, 1986.

Super, D.E.: *The Psychology of Careers*. New York: Harper & Row, 1957.

Super, D.E., Kowalski, R.S., and Gotkin, E.H.: *Floundering and Trial After High School*. New York: Teachers College, Columbia University, 1967 (mimeo).

Taylor, M.S.: 'The Roles of Occupational Knowledge and Vocational Self-Concept Crystalization in Students' School to Work Transition'. *Journal of Counseling Psychology*, Vol.32, 1985, pp. 539–550.

Thomas, R.: 'Guidance Interviews, Job Choice and Early Employment Careers'. In Office of Population Census and Surveys: *Starting Work and After*. n.d. (Cited in Clarke, L.: *The Practice of Vocational Guidance: a Critical Review of Research in the United Kingdom*. London: HMSO, 1981.)

Titley, R.W., and Titley, B.J.: 'Initial Choice of College Major: Are Only the Undecided Undecided?' *Journal of College Student Personnel*, Vol.21 No.3, 1980, pp. 292–298.

Unit for the Development of Adult Continuing Education: *The Challenge of Change*. Leicester: UDACE, 1986.

Wankowski, J.: 'Statistics and Economics of Educational Counselling in One University'. *British Journal of Guidance and Counselling*, Vol.7 No.1, 1979, pp. 31–41.

Watts, A.G.: 'The Impact of the "New Right": Policy Challenges Confronting Careers Guidance in England and Wales'. *British Journal of Guidance and Counselling*, Vol.19 No.3, September 1991, pp. 230–245.

Watts, A.G., and Herr, E.L.: 'Career(s) Education in Britain and the USA: Contrasts and Common Problems'. *British Journal of Guidance and Counselling*, Vol.4 No.2, July 1976, pp. 129–142.

References

Watts, A.G., Dartois, C., and Plant, P.: *Educational and Vocational Guidance Services for the 14–25 Age-Group in the European Community*. Maastricht: Presses Interuniversitaires Européennes, 1988.

West, M., and Newton, P.: *The Transition from School to Work*. Beckenham: Croom Helm, 1982.

White, M.: *Long-Term Unemployment and Labour Markets*. London: Policy Studies Institute, 1983.

White, M., and McRae, S.: *Young Adults in Long-Term Unemployment*. London: Policy Studies Institute, 1989.

Williamson, E.G., and Bordin, E.S.: 'Evaluating Counseling by Means of a Control-Group Experiment'. *School and Society*, Vol.52, 1940, pp. 434–440.

Williamson, P.: *Early Careers of 1970 Graduates*. Research Paper No.26. Department of Employment, 1981.